Unit 19: Into the Wo...

Unit Description:

God's plan to save people from sin came into sharper focus as Jesus was born at last. When Jesus grew up, He began His mission to bring people back to God. From the beginning, Jesus proved that He is the Son of God and that all that was written about Him by the prophets was true.

Unit 20: Prepare the Way

Unit Description:

Jesus grew up and began to prepare for His ministry. When Jesus was baptized, God confirmed His sonship. Jesus was subsequently tempted by Satan, but He did not sin.

Unit 21: Among the People

Unit Description:

As Jesus traveled throughout Judea, His personal encounters with ordinary people changed their lives in extraordinary ways. Jesus revealed that He was God the Son in human form, living among God's people and bringing salvation in Him alone.

Unit 19 · Session 1
From Adam to Jesus

BIBLE PASSAGE:
Matthew 1; Luke 3; John 1

STORY POINT:
Jesus' family line proved
He is the Messiah.

KEY PASSAGE:
John 1:1-2

BIG PICTURE QUESTION:
Is Jesus God or a human? As
the Son of God, Jesus is both
fully God and fully human.

INTRODUCE THE STORY
(10–15 MINUTES)
PAGE 6

→

TEACH THE STORY
(25–30 MINUTES)
PAGE 8

→

APPLY THE STORY
(25–30 MINUTES)
PAGE 14

Additional resources are available at gospelproject.com. For free training and
session-by-session help, visit Ministrygrid.com/thegospelproject.

LEADER Bible Study

The prophecies concerning Jesus' birth are numerous, and many of them refer to Jesus' lineage. Old Testament prophecies tell of the promised Messiah being born from the seed of a woman (Gen. 3:15); from the seed of Abraham (Gen. 22:18), Isaac (Gen. 21:12), and Jacob (Num. 24:17); from the tribe of Judah (Micah 5:2); from the line of Jesse (Isa. 11:1); and from the house of David (Jer. 23:5). The prophecies said He would be born of a virgin (Isa. 7:14) and would be the Son of God (1 Chron. 17:13-14; Ps. 2:7). Jesus fulfilled all of these prophecies.

In Bible times, Jews took great care to accurately record family genealogies. The family a person belonged to was directly linked to property rights. Matthew 1:1-17 and Luke 3:23-38 both chronicle the genealogy of Jesus. The account in Matthew presents Jesus as the king of the Jews—the legal heir to the throne of David. The account in Luke was written to Greek Christians and focuses on Jesus' descent from Adam.

Jesus was born as a baby in Bethlehem. He had earthly parents—Mary and Joseph—but His true Father is God. Jesus is fully God and fully man.

As fully God, "the entire fullness of God's nature dwells bodily in Christ" (Col. 2:9). As fully man, Jesus has a human body, human mind, and human emotions. (See Luke 2:7,52; Matt. 26:38.) He is our sinless representative (2 Cor. 5:21), sympathetic high priest (Heb. 4:15), and substitute sacrifice (1 John 4:10).

Use this Bible story with the kids you teach to review Jesus' ancestors and their stories in the Old Testament. Help kids recognize that God had been working out His plan to send Jesus over hundreds of years—through Adam, Abraham, Isaac, Rahab, Ruth, David, and others. God sent His Son to earth to save people from their sins.

The **BIBLE** Story

From Adam to Jesus

Matthew 1; Luke 3; John 1

Before He came to earth as a human being, **God the Son** was with the Father. No one created Him; He **has always existed.** God created the first people, Adam and Eve, but they did not obey Him. **All along, God planned to send His Son to earth to save people from sin. At just the right time, Jesus came to earth as a baby.** He was born to Mary, the wife of Joseph. **Jesus is different than any other baby who was ever born because He is fully God and fully human. Like all people on earth, Jesus' family had a history—a family tree.** Jesus had parents, grandparents, great-grandparents, and great-great-grandparents … back and back for many generations. **Jesus was born into the family of Abraham and the family of King David. Abraham had a son named Isaac. When Isaac had a family, one of his sons was named Jacob. Jacob was part of Jesus' family. Years later, a man named Salmon** (SAL mahn) **was born into Jesus' family tree. He married Rahab** (RAY hab), who hid the Israelite spies when they came to Jericho. **Rahab had a baby named Boaz** (BOH az). **Boaz** was a farmer, and he **married Ruth. Boaz and Ruth had a son named**

Obed (OH bed).

Obed's son was Jesse. Jesse had many sons; his youngest was David. David was just a boy when he was chosen to be Israel's king. King David liked to write. He wrote songs—called psalms—and some of them were about the time when Jesus would come to earth.

Other people in Jesus' family were kings too. **David's son Solomon was a king. King Jehoshaphat** (jih HAHSH uh fat) **was part of Jesus' family, and so was Uzziah** (uh ZIGH uh)**, Ahaz** (AY haz)**, Hezekiah** (HEZ ih kigh uh)**, and Josiah.**

God's people returned home from exile in Babylon. **Then Shealtiel** (shih AL tih el) **was born. His son was Zerubbabel** (zuh RUHB uh buhl)**. Later, Matthan** (MAT than) **came along. Matthan's son was named Jacob, and Jacob's son was named Joseph. Joseph is the man who married Jesus' mother, Mary. Joseph raised Jesus as his own son. Jesus was truly God's Son—the Messiah.**

Christ Connection: Jesus came to earth as a human. Jesus had earthly parents, Mary and Joseph, but His true Father is God. Through Jesus, God kept His promises to Abraham and David. Jesus saves people from their sins and adopts them into God's family.

John 1:1-2 (NIV)

In the beginning was the Word, and the Word was with God, and the Word was God. He was with God in the beginning.

Bible Storytelling Tips

• **Display art:** Show art from previous Bible stories and point out people from the Bible story.
• **Show name tags:** Write names from the Bible story on adhesive labels. Display the names as you tell the story.

INTRODUCE the Story

SESSION TITLE: From Adam to Jesus
BIBLE PASSAGE: Matthew 1; Luke 3; John 1
STORY POINT: Jesus' family line proved He is the Messiah.
KEY PASSAGE: John 1:1-2
BIG PICTURE QUESTION: Is Jesus God or a human? As the Son of God, Jesus is both fully God and fully human.

Welcome time

Tip: Be sensitive to kids who may be from difficult family backgrounds.

Greet each kid as he or she arrives. Use this time to collect the offering, fill out attendance sheets, and help new kids connect to your group. Prompt kids to dicuss their families.

SAY • Each of us has a different family. No matter what our families look like, God can use our families to help us learn and grow. Today we will learn about Jesus' family. Jesus is fully human and fully God. Because He is fully human, he had a human family!

Activity page (5 minutes)

· "Family Portrait" activity page, 1 per kid
· pencils or markers

Invite kids to complete the "Family Portrait" activity page. Kids will draw pictures of their families, or what they think their families might look like when they grow up and start their own.

SAY • God has given us all kinds of families. No family is perfect, but every family can be used by God to bless us and teach us about Him. Jesus had a family too! He was born as a human baby into a human family. We'll learn more about Jesus' family today.

Session starter (10 minutes)

OPTION 1: Never ending

Invite the kids to sit in a circle. Teach them a simple song that repeats over and over again. Consider using the following lyrics sung to the tune of "Row, Row, Row Your Boat."

> This song never ends;
> It goes on and on.
> If you start to sing it now,
> We'll sing from dusk till dawn.

SAY • Eventually, that song had to end, even though we said it wouldn't. And that song had a beginning too. Jesus isn't like this song. Jesus, the Son of God, has no beginning or end because He is fully God. But Jesus' life as a human did have a beginning and a family history too! We'll learn more about that today.

LOW PREP

Tip: You may lead the kids to sing the song as a round.

OPTION 2: Domino effects

Help the kids work in groups of three or four to set up various patterns of dominoes. Instruct the kids to take turns pushing over the first domino to observe what happens. Challenge them to make many patterns and see if there are any patterns that won't all fall down when the first domino is pushed.

· dominoes

SAY • Each domino that fell led right into the next. In a way, that's kind of like our families. Each set of parents had kids, leading to the next generation. Jesus had a human family just like we do. His family can be traced back very far. Let's learn more about it.

Transition to teach the story

TEACH the Story

SESSION TITLE: From Adam to Jesus
BIBLE PASSAGE: Matthew 1; Luke 3; John 1
STORY POINT: Jesus' family line proved He is the Messiah.
KEY PASSAGE: John 1:1-2
BIG PICTURE QUESTION: Is Jesus God or a human? As the Son of God, Jesus is both fully God and fully human.

· room decorations
· Theme Background Slide (optional)

Suggested Theme Decorating Ideas: Decorate the room to look like a photography studio. Make pastel colored backgrounds by painting and hanging sheets, use windshield sun-shades as reflector panels, and place a tripod near the middle of the stage. You may display the theme background slide.

Countdown

· countdown video

Show the countdown video as you transition to teach the story. Set it to end as the session begins.

Introduce the session (3 minutes)

· leader attire
· camera on a strap

[Leader enters wearing casual clothing and carrying a camera on a strap.]

Tip: If you prefer not to use themed content or characters, adapt or omit this introduction.

LEADER • Hey there. You must be my *[time]* o'clock appointment. Wow, there sure are a lot of you. It will be tough to get picture with all of you at once, but I'm a professional photographer, so I'll find a way to make it happen. Everyone stand up for the picture!

Let's see. *[Gesture to left side of the room]* I need you all to squeeze in a bit. And ... *[gesture to kids in the back]* Can I get you to stand up a little taller? In the front, can you all take a knee? Perfect. *[Hold up the camera.*]One, two, say cheese … three! [*Take, or pretend to take, a picture*]. Well done. Y'all are certainly very photogenic.

Are you all family, or just good friends? [*Allow responses*]. I had a feeling that might be the case. I take a lot of family photos, but this group seemed a bit large to all be blood relatives! You know who had a big family? Jesus! I don't just mean His immediate family, though. Jesus had a family that stretched back a long, long way.

Big picture question (1 minute)

LEADER • As we get to our story, I have a big picture question that I want you to think about. ***Is Jesus God or a human?*** It may seem like an easy question at first, but I want you to think about not just what the right answer is, but what that answer means. Our story should help shed some light on things.

Giant timeline (1 minute)

Show the giant timeline. Point to individual Bible stories as you review. · Giant Timeline

LEADER • We have been studying the Bible starting in the very beginning. God created the heavens and the earth, and everything God created was good. But you don't have to look far to see that things are not perfect like they were in the beginning.

Adam and Eve, the first humans, chose to disobey God. Sin entered the world and ever since then, everything has been messed up. But all along God had a plan to fix what sin broke. God planned to send a Rescuer. By the end of the Old Testament,

Into the World

the promised Rescuer still had not arrived, but God's plans had all been laid out. Today we will look back to see how Jesus' family had been chosen by God to prepare the world for His coming.

Tell the Bible story (10 minutes)

Open your Bible to Matthew 1; Luke 3; John 1. Use the Bible storytelling tips on the Bible story page to help you tell the story, or show the Bible story video "From Adam to Jesus."

LEADER • Since the beginning of creation, God's plan was working in the lives of His people. Adam had kids, who had kids, who had kids and so on all the way down the line. Abraham, Isaac, Jacob and Judah were all Jesus' ancestors. Ruth had Obed, who had Jesse, whose son David became a king. King David and his son Solomon, and Solomon's sons and grandsons and great-grandsons were all leading up to the perfect King, Jesus.

Jesus' family was chosen and guided by God in a special way. God told prophets to pay attention to this family because eventually this family led to the birth of Jesus, God the Son. **Jesus' family line proved He is the Messiah**.

So let's answer our question: *Is Jesus God or a human?* Jesus has a fully human family just like you and I, because Jesus is fully human. However, unlike us, Jesus is also fully God. *As the Son of God, Jesus is both fully God and fully human*. Jesus has always existed with God the Father and God the Holy Spirit. Jesus was raised by Joseph, but His Father is God.

- Bibles
- "From Adam to Jesus" video
- Big Picture Question Poster
- Bible Story Picture Poster
- Story Point Poster

Jesus' family was not a list of perfect people. All of Jesus' ancestors were sinners, just like we are and just like our ancestors were. Even so, God used them in His miraculous plan to bring forgiveness to sinners. God can use us and our families in incredible ways too, especially when we have faith in Jesus and obey Him out of love.

Christ connection

LEADER • Jesus came to earth as a human. Jesus had earthly parents, Mary and Joseph, but His true Father is God. Through Jesus, God kept His promises to Abraham and David. Jesus saves people from their sins and adopts them into God's family.

Note: You may use this opportunity to use Scripture and the guide provided to explain how to become a Christian. Make sure kids know when and where they can ask questions.

Questions from kids video (3 minutes)

Show the "Unit 19, Session 1" questions from kids video. Prompt kids to think about the differences and similarities between Adam and Jesus. Guide them to discuss how the family of God is different from our earthly families.

· "Unit 19, Session 1" Questions from Kids video

🌐 Missions moment (3 minutes)

Play the missions video "São Paulo Presents."

LEADER • We've learned that **Jesus' family line proved He was the Messiah**. Missionaries, like those in São Paulo, Brazil, want everyone to know Jesus, the Messiah, personally. When people trust in Jesus, they become our brothers and sisters in Christ!

Invite a kid to pray for the people in Brazil or for missionaries your church supports.

· "São Paulo Presents" missions video
· world map (optional)

Key passage (5 minutes)

· Key Passage Poster
· "The Word Was God (John 1:1-2)" song

Show the key passage poster. Lead the boys and girls to read together John 1:1-2. Then sing "The Word Was God (John 1:1-2)."

LEADER • Our key passage tells us that the Word was was God, and the Word was with God. The Word is Jesus. We know this is true because later in John 1 we learn that the Word became flesh and lived with us on earth, just as Jesus did. This verse helps us know more about who Jesus is. *Is Jesus God or a human? As the Son of God, Jesus is both fully God and fully human.*

Sing (4 minutes)

· "Take It to the Lord" song

LEADER • Jesus came to earth as a human, with a human family, human emotions, and human desires. He faced temptations, sadness, and pain just as we do. But He never sinned. He is the perfect Savior, and the best friend we could ever have. Let us worship Him together.

Sing together "Take It to the Lord."

Pray (2 minutes)

Invite kids to pray before dismissing to apply the story.

LEADER • Father, thank You for sending Your perfect Son to live a perfect life and die the death we deserve. Help us to see Jesus, the Word made flesh, more clearly today. Help us love Him more and obey Him better. Amen.

Dismiss to apply the story

The Gospel: God's Plan for Me

Ask kids if they have ever heard the word *gospel*. Clarify that the word *gospel* means "good news." It is the message about Christ, the kingdom of God, and salvation. Use the following guide to share the gospel with kids.

God rules. Explain to kids that the Bible tells us God created everything, and He is in charge of everything. Invite a volunteer to read Genesis 1:1 from the Bible. Read Revelation 4:11 or Colossians 1:16-17 aloud and explain what these verses mean.

We sinned. Tell kids that since the time of Adam and Eve, everyone has chosen to disobey God. (Romans 3:23) The Bible calls this sin. Because God is holy, God cannot be around sin. Sin separates us from God and deserves God's punishment of death. (Romans 6:23)

God provided. Choose a child to read John 3:16 aloud. Say that God sent His Son, Jesus, the perfect solution to our sin problem, to rescue us from the punishment we deserve. It's something we, as sinners, could never earn on our own. Jesus alone saves us. Read and explain Ephesians 2:8-9.

Jesus gives. Share with kids that Jesus lived a perfect life, died on the cross for our sins, and rose again. Because Jesus gave up His life for us, we can be welcomed into God's family for eternity. This is the best gift ever! Read Romans 5:8; 2 Corinthians 5:21; or 1 Peter 3:18.

We respond. Tell kids that they can respond to Jesus. Read Romans 10:9-10,13. Review these aspects of our response: Believe in your heart that Jesus alone saves you through what He's already done on the cross. Repent, turning from self and sin to Jesus. Tell God and others that your faith is in Jesus.

Offer to talk with any child who is interested in responding to Jesus. Provide *I'm a Christian Now!* for new Christians to take home and complete with their families.

APPLY the Story

SESSION TITLE: From Adam to Jesus

BIBLE PASSAGE: Matthew 1; Luke 3; John 1

STORY POINT: Jesus' family line proved He is the Messiah.

KEY PASSAGE: John 1:1-2

BIG PICTURE QUESTION: Is Jesus God or a human? As the Son of God, Jesus is both fully God and fully human.

Key passage activity (5 minutes)

- Key Passage Poster
- paper, 10 sheets
- pens or markers
- tape
- beanbag

Write each word or phrase from the key passage onto 10 sheets of paper. Use tape to fix the sheets to the floor in a hopscotch pattern. Instruct the kids to line up and take turns tossing a beanbag onto the key passage before hopping across the passage, saying each word aloud. Kids will skip the word on which the beanbag landed.

SAY • Our key passage comes from the very beginning of the Gospel of John. John wrote to tell people about Jesus. Jesus is the Word of God; through Jesus, all things exist. Jesus perfectly represents God's desire for the world. John also explains that the Word is God and is with God. *Is Jesus God or a human? As the Son of God, Jesus is both fully God and fully human*.

Discussion & Bible skills (10 minutes)

- Bibles, 1 per kid
- Story Point Poster
- Small Group Timeline and Map Set (005802970, optional)

Distribute a Bible to each kid. Help kids find Matthew 1; Luke 3; John 1. Explain that these books are in the Gospels division of the New Testament. These books, along with Mark, tell the story of Jesus' life and ministry on earth, including His death and resurrection.

Ask the following questions. Lead the group to discuss:

Option: Retell or review the Bible story using the bolded text of the Bible story script.

1. Where was Jesus before He was born as a human baby? (*with God the Father, John 1:1*)
2. Who were three of the women named in Jesus' family line? (*Rahab, Ruth, and Mary; Matt. 1:5,16*)
3. Who was Jesus' earthly father? (*Joseph, Luke 3:23*)
4. Why is it important to understand who was part of Jesus' family? *Guide kids to understand that many of God's promises about the coming Messiah had to do with specific families. Abraham, Isaac, and Jacob were promised blessings to bless the world; and David was promised a descendant who would reign forever. Seeing Jesus' family line helps us understand that Jesus is the Messiah.*
5. How do you feel knowing Jesus' family was not perfect? *Discuss the idea that God uses imperfect people to bring about His perfect plans. Jesus' family was not perfect, our families are not perfect, and we are not perfect. Even so, God can use us in His plans.*
6. How can we be a part of God's family? *Remind kids that Jesus' death and resurrection made the way for us to be forgiven of sin and adopted into God's family. Even though people in God's family are not perfect, we can love one another and help one another with God's power and help. Someday all believers will be perfected at Jesus' return and the restoration of the world.*

SAY • **Jesus' family line proved He is the Messiah**. His family was not perfect, but God used them to bring our perfect Savior into the world. Jesus died on the cross to make the way for us to be in God's family.

LOW PREP

· pictures of local landmarks (optional)
· map of your city (optional)

Tip: Use this activity option to reinforce the missions moment found in Teach the Story.

Activity choice (10 minutes)

OPTION 1: Local landmarks

Show pictures of or describe local landmarks that your group would be familiar with, such as a tourist attraction, famous restaurant, amusement park, or statue. Talk about why those places or things are important to your community.

SAY • In the video about São Paulo, we saw a few things that seem important to the people there: music, art, and food. When missionaries move to a new city, they want to get to know the people and places. They learn about things like the local music and food because they want to make new friends. They will tell their friends about Jesus, the Messiah, so that more families will know Him.

When people visit our city, they may go to the places we talked about. Those might be good places for us to meet new people to tell them about Jesus. We can live on mission by loving other people and telling them the gospel.

· Bibles
· Giant Timeline and Family Line of Jesus Posters (005802967, optional)

OPTION 2: Family history

Select five or six people from Jesus' family lineage about whom your kids have learned. Challenge the kids to work together to retell stories they know about those people. Provide Bibles and help the kids find the passages the stories come from. You may also use the "Family Line of Jesus" posters included with the giant timeline.

Suggested people:
• Abraham (Gen. 22)
• Jacob (Gen. 27)
• Rahab (Josh. 2)

- Ruth (Ruth 3)
- David (2 Sam. 7)
- Zerubbabel (Ezra 3)

SAY • When we look back at the Old Testament, we read story after story of God using imperfect people to bring about His perfect plan. All along the way, God was planning to send the Messiah, our perfect Rescuer. **Jesus' family line proved He is the Messiah**. But God the Son existed before He was born as a human. He has always existed. *Is Jesus God or a human? As the Son of God, Jesus is both fully God and fully human*.

Reflection and prayer (5 minutes)

Distribute a sheet of paper to each child. Ask the kids to write about or draw a picture to answer the following questions:

- What does this story teach me about God or about the gospel?
- What does this story teach me about myself?
- Whom can I tell about this story?

Make sure to send the sheets home with kids alongside the activity page so that parents can see what their kids have been learning.

If time remains, take prayer requests or allow kids to complete the Bible story coloring page provided with this session. Pray for your group.

· pencils and crayons
· paper
· Bible Story Coloring Page, 1 per kid

Tip: Give parents this week's *Big Picture Cards for Families* to allow families to interact with the biblical content at home.

Unit 19 · Session 2
John Was Born

BIBLE PASSAGE:
Luke 1

STORY POINT:
John was born to prepare
the way for Jesus.

KEY PASSAGE:
John 1:1-2

BIG PICTURE QUESTION:
Is Jesus God or a human? As
the Son of God, Jesus is both
fully God and fully human.

INTRODUCE THE STORY	**TEACH THE STORY**	**APPLY THE STORY**
(10–15 MINUTES)	(25–30 MINUTES)	(25–30 MINUTES)
PAGE 22	PAGE 24	PAGE 30

 → →

Additional resources are available at gospelproject.com. For free training and
session-by-session help, visit Ministrygrid.com/thegospelproject.

LEADER Bible Study

Some of the last words of the Lord recorded in the Old Testament are found in Malachi 4: "Look, I am going to send you the prophet Elijah … he will turn the hearts of fathers to their children and the hearts of children to their fathers" (vv. 5-6). The Book of Malachi was written more than 400 years before Jesus was born. For centuries, God's people did not hear from Him. They were back in their homeland but were subject to other ruling nations. Eventually, the Romans took over.

The Roman emperor installed Herod as a leader over Judea and surrounding regions such as Samaria and Galilee. To gain the people's favor, King Herod replaced Zerubbabel's temple in Jerusalem with a beautiful marble temple constructed by 10,000 workers. This was the temple in which Zechariah, a priest from the family of Abijah, served the Lord. This was the temple in which God, through the angel Gabriel, broke His silence after so many years.

Zechariah and his wife, Elizabeth, were both "righteous in God's sight" (Luke 1:6), living by faith in God's promise to send a Messiah. Like Abraham and Sarah in Genesis 18, they were getting along in years and did not have any children. Elizabeth's barrenness was a point of disgrace for her among the community (Luke 1:25) and God graciously answered this couple's prayers.

An angel appeared to Zechariah in the temple sanctuary and delivered good news: "Your prayer has been heard. Your wife Elizabeth will bear a son." Echoing Malachi's prophecy, the angel declared this son would "turn the hearts of fathers to their children" (Luke 1:17)

For his doubting, Zechariah was rendered mute until the promise came to pass. When John was born, Zechariah could speak again. He praised God and prophesied. John was born to prepare the way for Jesus. John would point people to Jesus, the Savior God promised.

The **BIBLE** Story

John Was Born
Luke 1

Zechariah and his wife, Elizabeth, were old and had no children. They lived outside of Jerusalem in the hill country and **did what was right.** Zechariah was a priest and at that time, King Herod ruled over Judea. **Twice a year, Zechariah went to the temple in Jerusalem to carry out his duties as a priest.** Many priests served in the temple. **One day, Zechariah was chosen to go into the sanctuary of the Lord and burn incense.** People gathered outside to pray, and Zechariah went inside the sanctuary. **Suddenly, an angel of the Lord appeared. Zechariah was terrified!**

"Do not be afraid, Zechariah," the angel said. **"God heard your prayer. Your wife will have a son, and you will name him John.** His birth will bring you joy. God will be with Him. The Holy Spirit will fill him even before he is born."

The angel said that John would help many people turn back to God. John would go ahead of the Lord and get people ready for His coming.

Zechariah asked the angel, "How can I know this will happen? I'm old, and my wife is old."

The angel said, "God sent me to tell you this good news. Because

you did not believe my words, you won't be able to speak until these things happen."

Zechariah left the temple. The people outside realized he had seen a vision and could not talk. When he was done serving in Jerusalem, **Zechariah went home to Elizabeth. In time, she became pregnant and gave birth to a son.** Her neighbors and relatives rejoiced.

Zechariah and Elizabeth named their son John. Suddenly, Zechariah could speak again. He began praising God. The people who lived nearby could tell that God was with John. **The Holy Spirit filled John. Zechariah praised God and told the people God's words: "God has come to help His people. He will save us through David's family. He will rescue us from our enemies."** Then he spoke to John: "And you will be called a prophet of the Most High. You will go before the Lord to prepare the way for Him."

The time had come. God was going to bring His light into the darkness of the world. Peace was coming for God's people.

John grew up and lived in the wilderness until God called him to get the people ready for Jesus.

Christ Connection: When Zechariah believed God's word, he praised God. John was born to prepare the way for Jesus. John would point people to Jesus, and they would praise God for keeping His promise to send the Savior.

Bible Storytelling Tips

• **Make eye contact:** As you tell the story, make eye contact with kids to draw them in. Pause at appropriate points to build anticipation when the angel appears to Zechariah.
• **Dress in costume:** Wear Bible times clothes as you tell the story. Act out the role of Zechariah.

INTRODUCE the Story

SESSION TITLE: John Was Born
BIBLE PASSAGE: Luke 1
STORY POINT: John was born to prepare the way for Jesus.
KEY PASSAGE: John 1:1-2
BIG PICTURE QUESTION: Is Jesus God or a human? As the Son of God, Jesus is both fully God and fully human.

Welcome time

Greet each kid as he or she arrives. Use this time to collect the offering, fill out attendance sheets, and help new kids connect to your group. Prompt kids to talk about what they want to be when they grow up.

SAY • Believe it or not, many adults end up working very different jobs from what they thought they wanted to do when they were your age. God works through all situations, even when we have jobs we didn't expect. But today we will learn about a baby whose job and purpose was set before he was even born!

Activity page (5 minutes)

· "Baby or Maybe"
activity page,
1 per kid
· pencils or markers

Invite kids to complete the "Baby or Maybe" activity page. Kids will circle items they think are necessary to care for a baby, draw boxes around the items that are helpful but not necessary, and cross out items that are unnecessary.

SAY • Nowadays, lots of different inventions can help us care for babies. In our story today, we will learn about a time God sent an angel to tell a man about a baby his wife would have. What might they have done to prepare?

Session starter (10 minutes)

OPTION 1: Zipped lips

Task your group with completing a challenge, such as lining up by age, acting out their favorite TV show, or using their bodies to make different shapes on the ground. Inform the kids that they may not speak while completing the challenge.

SAY • Wow, that was difficult! We spend a lot of time speaking to communicate, and it's tough to get our ideas across without talking. Today, we will learn about a man who doubted God and couldn't speak until God kept His promise to send a baby boy. How would you feel if you couldn't speak for nine months?

OPTION 2: A job to do

Gather the kids to sit in a circle. Show the different tools or pictures of tools and ask the kids to raise their hands if they know what the tool is designed to do. Call on a kid and let her describe the tool and what it does. Suggested tools: hammer, soup ladle, padlock, pencil

· tools or pictures of tools

Tip: For a fun twist, challenge the kids to come up with additional uses for each tool.

SAY • Each of those tools was designed with a specific job or purpose in mind. A hammer is great for pounding in nails, but it wouldn't work well for serving soup. Today we will learn about a baby boy whom God had big plans for. When this boy grew up, God used him to prepare the way for the Messiah. How might someone prepare the way for the Messiah?

Transition to teach the story

TEACH the Story

SESSION TITLE: John Was Born
BIBLE PASSAGE: Luke 1
STORY POINT: John was born to prepare the way for Jesus.
KEY PASSAGE: John 1:1-2
BIG PICTURE QUESTION: Is Jesus God or a human? As the Son of God, Jesus is both fully God and fully human.

Countdown

· countdown video

Show the countdown video as you transition to teach the story. Set it to end as the session begins.

Introduce the session (3 minutes)

· leader attire
· camera on a strap

[Leader enters wearing casual clothing and carrying a camera on a strap.]

LEADER • Hey, everyone! Welcome back to my studio. Can I tell you a little secret? It's really hard to take baby pictures. I don't mean it's hard to take the pictures; babies don't move all that fast, so it's fairly simple to capture their image on film. But it can be really hard to get good pictures of babies. You know, where the baby is smiling and happy? Some babies just don't want to smile sometimes.

Tip: If you prefer not to use themed content or characters, adapt or omit this introduction.

In fact, I just got done with a set of baby pictures for a friend of mine. Their daughter is absolutely precious. She's got the biggest brown eyes and cute chubby cheeks. But today? It didn't matter what I did, she did not want to smile. I spent hours squeezing toys and waving teddy bears and whistling wildly. All I have to show for it are eight dozen pictures of the grumpiest baby you've ever seen. Don't get me wrong; they are still adorable pictures, but she isn't smiling in a single one!

All this talk of babies makes me think of a Bible story. God had big plans for a baby boy and sent an angel to tell about those plans. But the baby's dad didn't believe at first! I'll tell you all about it.

Big picture question (1 minute)

LEADER • To help us think through our story, let's remember the big picture question. *Is Jesus God or a human? As the Son of God, Jesus is both fully God and fully human*. It is important to understand this because it helps us see that Jesus alone can unite us to God. Jesus experienced the same kinds of temptations, frustrations, and pains as we do but never sinned. He also has all the power and majesty of God and is worthy of worship. Only Jesus could have died for our sins to make the way for us to live forever with God.

Giant timeline (1 minute)

Show the giant timeline. Point to individual Bible stories as you review.

· Giant Timeline

LEADER • Through the entire Old Testament, the history of God's people pointed forward to the time when God would fulfill His promise to send a Rescuer. We learned last week that **Jesus' family line proved He is the Messiah**. This week, we will learn about a special baby who would come right before Jesus did to prepare the way for Jesus.

Tell the Bible story (10 minutes)

· Bibles
· "John Was Born"
  video
· Big Picture Question
  Poster
· Bible Story Picture
  Poster
· Story Point Poster

Open your Bible to Luke 1. Use the Bible storytelling tips on the Bible story page to help you tell the story, or show the Bible story video "John Was Born."

LEADER • At the very end of the Old Testament, the last prophet, Malachi, wrote about a messenger who would prepare the way for the Messiah. John was the messenger whom God had promised through Malachi.

Zechariah did not believe the angel Gabriel at first. Zechariah knew that he and his wife were too old to have children. However, one wonderful thing about God is that He has power over all things. Nothing can stop His plans, and He often does things no one else could do to prove His power and love.

Despite their old age, Zechariah and Elizabeth had a baby just as God promised. God is faithful, and all His promises come true. John was filled with the power of the Holy Spirit even as a baby! God had plans for John, and John's birth was like a small glimpse at the birth of the Messiah still to come. **John was born to prepare the way for Jesus.**

Christ connection

Note: You may use this opportunity to use Scripture and the guide provided to explain how to become a Christian. Make sure kids know when and where they can ask questions.

LEADER • God used the lives of Zechariah, Elizabeth, and John to bring glory to Himself. Elizabeth should have been too old to have a baby, but God allowed her to have John anyway. When Zechariah believed God's word, he praised God. **John was born to prepare the way for Jesus.** John would point people to Jesus, and they would praise God for keeping His promise to send the Savior. Ultimately, Jesus died on the cross and rose again to glorify God and make the way for us to be saved to glorify God as well.

Questions from kids video (3 minutes)

Show the "Unit 19, Session 2" questions from kids video. Prompt kids to think about who angels are and what they do. Guide them to discuss the special roles God has for people in His kingdom.

· "Unit 19, Session 2" Questions from Kids video

Missions moment (3 minutes)

Show the "Relentless Love (Part 1)" missions video.

LEADER • **John was born to prepare the way for Jesus.** Did you know that, in a way, you were born to prepare the way for people to know Jesus too? God wants us, no matter our age or where we live, to love Jesus and tell other people about Him. In Brazil, missionaries are preparing the way for people in São Paulo to know about Jesus.

Pray for missionaries in Brazil or for missionaries your church supports.

· "Relentless Love (Part 1)" missions video

Key passage (5 minutes)

Show the key passage poster. Lead the boys and girls to read together John 1:1-2. Then sing the key passage song.

LEADER • Our key passage comes from the very start of the Gospel of John. The writer of this book was not the same John from our story today, but one of Jesus' closest friends and disciples. He explained that Jesus is God and was with God in the beginning. That means that even before Jesus was born as a baby, He already existed eternally with God the Father and God the Spirit. *Is Jesus God or a human? As the Son*

· Key Passage Poster
· "The Word Was God (John 1:1-2)" song

of God, Jesus is both fully God and fully human.

Sing (4 minutes)

· "Jesus Messiah" song

LEADER • Since even before the creation of the world, God had planned to send Jesus to save people from sin. Jesus is the Messiah, and He is worthy of all our praise.

Sing together "Jesus Messiah."

Pray (2 minutes)

Invite kids to pray before dismissing to apply the story.

LEADER • Father, thank You for Your love. Only You are able to do all things, and only You are worthy of all praise. Help us love and obey You. You sent Your only Son to save us from sin, and we want to glorify You with our lives. Amen.

Dismiss to apply the story

The Gospel: God's Plan for Me

Ask kids if they have ever heard the word *gospel*. Clarify that the word *gospel* means "good news." It is the message about Christ, the kingdom of God, and salvation. Use the following guide to share the gospel with kids.

God rules. Explain to kids that the Bible tells us God created everything, and He is in charge of everything. Invite a volunteer to read Genesis 1:1 from the Bible. Read Revelation 4:11 or Colossians 1:16-17 aloud and explain what these verses mean.

We sinned. Tell kids that since the time of Adam and Eve, everyone has chosen to disobey God. (Romans 3:23) The Bible calls this sin. Because God is holy, God cannot be around sin. Sin separates us from God and deserves God's punishment of death. (Romans 6:23)

God provided. Choose a child to read John 3:16 aloud. Say that God sent His Son, Jesus, the perfect solution to our sin problem, to rescue us from the punishment we deserve. It's something we, as sinners, could never earn on our own. Jesus alone saves us. Read and explain Ephesians 2:8-9.

Jesus gives. Share with kids that Jesus lived a perfect life, died on the cross for our sins, and rose again. Because Jesus gave up His life for us, we can be welcomed into God's family for eternity. This is the best gift ever! Read Romans 5:8; 2 Corinthians 5:21; or 1 Peter 3:18.

We respond. Tell kids that they can respond to Jesus. Read Romans 10:9-10,13. Review these aspects of our response: Believe in your heart that Jesus alone saves you through what He's already done on the cross. Repent, turning from self and sin to Jesus. Tell God and others that your faith is in Jesus.

Offer to talk with any child who is interested in responding to Jesus. Provide *I'm a Christian Now!* for new Christians to take home and complete with their families.

APPLY the Story

SESSION TITLE: John Was Born

BIBLE PASSAGE: Luke 1

STORY POINT: John was born to prepare the way for Jesus.

KEY PASSAGE: John 1:1-2

BIG PICTURE QUESTION: Is Jesus God or a human? As the Son of God, Jesus is both fully God and fully human.

Key passage activity (5 minutes)

· Key Passage Poster
· string or twine
· marker
· clothespins, 15–20
· jar

Hang a length of string or twine across your room where kids can reach it. Write each word or phrase of the key passage on a separate clothespin and put the clothespins in a jar. Invite the kids to take turns drawing a clothespin and placing it on the string in the correct order. When kids finish drawing clothespins and ordering the verses, say them multiple times together.

SAY • John was one of Jesus' closest friends and disciples. He wrote the Book of John and started it all out by explaining who Jesus is. Jesus is God the Son and was with God the Father and God the Holy Spirit even at the very beginning. Though Jesus wasn't born as a human until many years after creation, He has always existed. *Is Jesus God or a human? As the Son of God, Jesus is both fully God and fully human*.

Discussion & Bible skills (10 minutes)

· Bibles, 1 per kid
· Story Point Poster
· Small Group Timeline and Map Set
   (005802970, optional)

Distribute a Bible to each kid. Help kids find Luke 1. Ask a volunteer to explain which division of the New Testament the Book of Luke can be found in (*the Gospels*) and what that division contains (*the stories of Jesus' life and ministry*).

Ask the following questions. Lead the group to discuss:

Option: Retell or review the Bible story using the bolded text of the Bible story script.

1. Where was Zechariah when Gabriel told him about John's birth? (*in the sanctuary of the Lord, Luke 1:8-10*)
2. Why was Zechariah unable to speak until John was born? (*He did not believe God at first, Luke 1:20*)
3. Where did John live when he grew up? (*in the wilderness, Luke 1:80*)
4. Can you think of times we doubt God, or struggle to understand how His plans work? *Guide kids to discuss how they feel about God in hard times. Remind kids that God is always faithful. No matter how we feel or what situations we face, God's promises are sure and will come true in His perfect timing. Help them understand that we can read our Bibles and pray to help us learn to trust God more.*
5. What are some ways God can use you to point people to Jesus? *Encourage kids to think about their friends and family members who may not love Jesus. Discuss ways to show them God's love and share the gospel with them. Remind kids that even people who know and love Jesus need to be pointed to Jesus to help them remember how good He is.*
6. When is it easy to praise God? When is it hard to? *Discuss with the kids how difficult times can make it hard to trust God, but they can also push us toward the Lord as we learn to rely on Him for support. Remind the kids that the Bible teaches we should praise God in good times and difficult times.*

SAY • **John was born to prepare the way for Jesus.** We can help prepare the way for Jesus by loving others.

Activity choice (10 minutes)

OPTION 1: Cinco Marias

Scatter the beanbags on the floor. Invite a kid to select one of the beanbags from the floor and pick it up. Instruct her to toss the beanbag into the air and try to grab one beanbag from the floor before catching the tossed beanbag. She will repeat this process until she has collected all the beanbags from the floor. Then re-scatter the beanbags and play again, allowing another kid to take a turn. After each kid has had a turn, challenge the kids to play a second round in which they must grab two beanbags each time they toss up the selected beanbag.

SAY • That was so fun! That's a game they play in Brazil called *Cinco Marias*, which means "five Marys." It's somewhat similar to a game that children in the United States play, called jacks. When we learn about other cultures, we are better able to make friendships with people from all over the world.

We can use our relationships with other people to glorify God by loving them well and telling them about Jesus. **John was born to prepare the way for Jesus**, and we can help prepare people to hear about Jesus too!

OPTION 2: Point the way

Instruct the kids to sit in a circle. Select a kid to stand outside the circle. He will close his eyes while you give a button or other small object to one of the kids in the circle. She will hide the button in her hand or underneath her. The goal of the kid whose eyes are closed will be to figure out who is hiding the button. Before he opens his eyes to do so, silently select a kid, who will always point to the correct

Tip: Use this activity option to reinforce the missions moment found in Teach the Story.

· button or other small object

kid. Inform the others that they may point to whomever they wish. Invite the first kid to open his eyes and look to see who is pointing to whom. Challenge him to guess who is hiding the button. Play additional rounds as time allows. Select new kids to hide and find the button, but ensure that the kid who always points correctly stays the same.

SAY • In that game, a lot of kids were pointing in different directions, but only one kid in each round was definitely pointing the right way.

John was born to prepare the way for Jesus. Everyone who listened to John was pointed in the right direction—toward Jesus. In our lives, we need to be sure the people we listen to and follow are pointing us in the right direction too—toward loving and obeying Jesus.

Reflection and prayer (5 minutes)

Distribute a sheet of paper to each child. Ask the kids to write about or draw a picture to answer the following questions:

· pencils and crayons
· paper
· Bible Story Coloring Page, 1 per kid

- What does this story teach me about God or about the gospel?
- What does this story teach me about myself?
- Whom can I tell about this story?

Make sure to send the sheets home with kids alongside the activity page so that parents can see what their kids have been learning.

If time remains, take prayer requests or allow kids to complete the Bible story coloring page provided with this session. Pray for your group.

Tip: Give parents this week's *Big Picture Cards for Families* to allow families to interact with the biblical content at home.

Use Week of:

Unit 19 · Session 3
Jesus Was Born

BIBLE PASSAGE:
Luke 2

STORY POINT:
Jesus was born to be God's
promised Savior.

KEY PASSAGE:
John 1:1-2

BIG PICTURE QUESTION:
Is Jesus God or a human? As
the Son of God, Jesus is both
fully God and fully human.

INTRODUCE THE STORY
(10–15 MINUTES)
PAGE 38

→

TEACH THE STORY
(25–30 MINUTES)
PAGE 40

→

APPLY THE STORY
(25–30 MINUTES)
PAGE 46

Additional resources are available at gospelproject.com. For free training and
session-by-session help, visit Ministrygrid.com/thegospelproject.

LEADER Bible Study

After the angel Gabriel appeared to Zechariah and predicted the birth of John—the forerunner of the Messiah—he appeared to Mary and predicted that she too would have a baby. This baby would be named Jesus, and He would be God's Son. "He will be great and will be called the Son of the Most High … His kingdom will have no end," Gabriel said. (See Luke 1:32-33.) Mary visited Zechariah and his wife, Elizabeth, who was pregnant with John. Inside the womb, John leaped for joy in the presence of Mary's unborn baby.

Mary and Joseph lived in Nazareth. When Caesar Augustus called for a census, they traveled to Bethlehem—the very place the Messiah was prophesied to be born. (Micah 5:2) There, in a stable, God the Son entered the world as a baby.

3

Imagine the shepherds' surprise when an angel of the Lord suddenly appeared. The Bible says that they were terrified! But the angel brought them good news: "Today in the city of David a Savior was born for you, who is the Messiah, the Lord" (Luke 2:11). This Savior—the long-awaited deliverer and redeemer—had come.

Not only did Jesus come into the world as the Savior, He came as our King. Some time after Jesus' birth, wise men came to worship Jesus. They brought Him gifts suitable for a king—gold, frankincense, and myrrh. Jesus is the King who will rule forever, just as God promised King David. (See 2 Sam. 7.)

When you share this story with kids, remind them that Jesus came because we needed Him. The purpose of Jesus' birth was twofold: to bring glory to God and to make peace between God and those who trust in Jesus' death and resurrection. Celebrating the birth of Jesus is about rejoicing over the greatest gift we could ever receive. God's own Son came to earth to be our Savior and our King.

The **BIBLE** Story

Jesus Was Born
Luke 2

Mary and Joseph lived in the town of **Nazareth. During the time Mary was pregnant, the Roman emperor**, Caesar Augustus, **announced that everyone needed to be registered** for a census. Since **Joseph** was a descendant of King David, he **and Mary traveled to Bethlehem**, the city of David.

While they were there, the time came for Mary to have her baby. Mary and Joseph looked for a safe place to stay, but every place was full. So Mary and Joseph found a place where animals were kept, and that is where Mary had her baby. Joseph named Him Jesus. Mary wrapped the baby tightly in cloth and laid Him in a feeding trough.

That night, some shepherds were watching over their sheep in the fields near Bethlehem. Suddenly, an angel stood before them and the glory of the Lord shone around them. They were terrified! **The angel said, "Don't be afraid! I have very good news for you and for all the people: Today a Savior, who is the Messiah and the Lord, was born for you in the city of David."** Then the angel said, **"You will find a baby wrapped tightly in cloth and lying in a manger."**

Suddenly, a whole army of angels appeared, praising God and saying, "Glory to God in the highest heaven, and peace on earth to people He favors!"

When the angels left and returned to heaven, **the shepherds** decided to go see if the angel's words were true. They **hurried to Bethlehem and found Mary and Joseph and the baby, who was lying in the feeding trough. Then the shepherds went and told others about the baby Jesus.** Everyone who heard about Jesus was surprised and amazed. Mary thought about everything that was happening and tried to understand it. **The shepherds returned to their fields, praising God because everything had happened just as the angel said.**

Christ Connection: The birth of Jesus was good news! Jesus was not an ordinary baby. He is God's Son, sent to earth from heaven. Jesus, the promised Savior, came into the world to deliver us from sin and death.

Bible Storytelling Tips

• **Use props:** As you tell the story, display a nativity scene. Allow kids to move the pieces around as you tell the story.
• **Adjust lighting:** Dim the lights to simulate a nighttime setting. Shine a bright light when describing the angel's appearance.

INTRODUCE the Story

SESSION TITLE: Jesus Was Born
BIBLE PASSAGE: Luke 2
STORY POINT: Jesus was born to be God's promised Savior.
KEY PASSAGE: John 1:1-2
BIG PICTURE QUESTION: Is Jesus God or a human? As the Son of God, Jesus is both fully God and fully human.

Welcome time

Greet each kid as he or she arrives. Use this time to collect the offering, fill out attendance sheets, and help new kids connect to your group. Prompt kids to discuss a time they made and kept a promise.

SAY • When we want someone to trust us, we might say that we promise to do something. Although we cannot perfectly keep every promise we might make, God can. He promised to send a Rescuer, and that's exactly what He did. Today we will learn about when Jesus was born.

Activity page (5 minutes)

· "Not Like the Others" activity page, 1 per kid
· pencils or markers

Invite kids to complete the "Not Like the Others" activity page. Kids will examine each set of three pictures and circle the item that does not belong in the set.

SAY • In that last set of pictures, it might have seemed the crown did not belong, but in a way, it could have. Jesus is the King of kings, and Jesus was born in a place where animals such as donkeys or cows are kept. So in a way, a donkey, a cow, and a crown do go together.

Session starter (10 minutes)

OPTION 1: Christmas charades

Invite the kids to take turns acting out something they associate with Christmas, such as twinkling lights, snow, cookies, or presents. Challenge the other kids to guess what the volunteer is acting out.

Tip: Guide kids away from secular or fantasy themed Christmas traditions.

SAY • It might seem odd that we are acting out Christmasy things, but it's because today we are learning about Jesus' birth! **Jesus was born to be God's promised Savior**. We usually celebrate Jesus' birth in December at Christmastime, but there's no wrong time to celebrate God's faithfulness to send a perfect Savior to rescue us from sin.

OPTION 2: Promises, promises

Instruct the kids to stand in a circle. Select a kid to start the game by saying "I promise I can … ," finishing the statement with a cool or unexpected action. Call on other kids to vote whether they think the kid can do it or not. If any kids think he cannot do what he promised, he must either prove he can do it, or sit out. If he can do it, the kids who challenged him must sit out.

SAY • That was a fun game, but some of you bluffed! You said you could do something you could not. God always tells the truth. He is always faithful and keeps all His promises. He promised to send a Rescuer, and today we will learn about how He did so.

Transition to teach the story

TEACH the Story

SESSION TITLE: Jesus Was Born
BIBLE PASSAGE: Luke 2
STORY POINT: Jesus was born to be God's promised Savior.
KEY PASSAGE: John 1:1-2
BIG PICTURE QUESTION: Is Jesus God or a human? As the Son of God, Jesus is both fully God and fully human.

Countdown

· countdown video

Show the countdown video as you transition to teach the story. Set it to end as the session begins.

Introduce the session (3 minutes)

· leader attire
· camera on a strap

[Leader enters wearing casual clothing and carrying a camera on a strap.]

Tip: If you prefer not to use themed content or characters, adapt or omit this introduction.

LEADER • Hey there, friends! I'm glad you could make it today. Last week I had a photo shoot to get some baby pictures for a friend of mine. Her baby is the cutest little girl, but I had trouble getting her to smile for the camera.

Well, this week, I promised I would try again, and in a few hours, I'm going to keep that promise. My friend and her baby girl are coming back in for round two. As I understand it, she's in a much better mood today, so I think we will get some good photographs.

It's a bit of a bummer that the baby isn't old enough to understand English yet; I have been reading about the birth of Jesus, and I think the story of the first Christmas is so joyful, anyone who understands it can't help but smile when thinking about it! In fact, let's see if that theory holds up. I want to tell you the story of Jesus' birth, and you let me know if it makes you want to smile.

Big picture question (1 minute)

LEADER • As we get into Jesus' birth, it's important to remember that Jesus' life as a human had a definite starting point when Mary became pregnant with Him. Even so, God the Son has always existed—since even before the creation of the world. That brings us to our big picture question and answer these last few weeks. *Is Jesus God or a human? As the Son of God, Jesus is both fully God and fully human.*

Jesus completely understands our feelings, thoughts, and temptations, because He has lived as a human. He also has all power and majesty and is worthy of all praise because He is God's Son.

Giant timeline (1 minute)

Show the giant timeline. Point to individual Bible stories as you review.

· Giant Timeline

LEADER • Two weeks ago, we learned that **Jesus' family line proved He is the Messiah**. God had promised to send a Rescuer through Abraham's family to be born into David's family as an eternal King. Last week, we learned about the birth of John, whom God used to fulfill Malachi's prophecy that a messenger would come before the Messiah. **John was born to prepare the way for Jesus**. This week, we will learn why Jesus was born as a human.

Tell the Bible story (10 minutes)

Open your Bible to Luke 2. Use the Bible storytelling tips on the Bible story page to help you tell the story, or show the Bible story video "Jesus Was Born."

LEADER • God always proves Himself faithful. Time and time again, God told His people that the Messiah was coming. Despite their continued sin and inability to obey, God remained faithful and kept His promise to send Jesus.

Despite our inability to ever earn God's love, He still loves us. God would have been justified and righteous to choose not to save people lost in sin, but instead He chose to send His only Son to become a human like us. Jesus is the King of kings, but He came to earth as a humble baby to ordinary people, and He was visited by lowly shepherds.

Everything about this story seems backwards from what people might have expected. A king born in a manger? The Creator and King of the universe in a helpless human body? *Is Jesus God or a human? As the Son of God, Jesus is both fully God and fully human*. God's faithfulness does not have to meet our expectations, and it is always much better than we could imagine. Jesus did not come to be served, but to serve. **Jesus was born to be God's promised Savior**.

Christ connection

LEADER • The birth of Jesus was good news! Jesus was not an ordinary baby. He is God's Son, sent to earth from heaven. Jesus, the promised Savior, came into the world to deliver us from sin and death. Although

- Bibles
- "Jesus Was Born" video
- Big Picture Question Poster
- Bible Story Picture Poster
- Story Point Poster

Note: You may use this opportunity to use Scripture and the guide provided to explain how to become a Christian. Make sure kids know when and where they can ask questions.

He is fully God, the Bible tells us that He humbled Himself to become fully human. He humbled Himself not just to become human, but to die the death we deserved. When we trust in Jesus, God forgives our sins and gives us eternal life with Him.

Questions from kids video (3 minutes)

Show the "Unit 19, Session 3" questions from kids video. Prompt kids to think about how we know Jesus is God's Son. Guide them to discuss whom they can tell about Jesus, God's Son.

- "Unit 19, Session 3" Questions from Kids video

Missions moment (3 minutes)

Display the "Brazilian Flag" printable and distribute copies of the "Brazil Facts" printable to four volunteers. Instruct them to take turns reading the facts, pausing when they get to the blank so kids can call out the word they think fits in the blank.

- "Brazilian Flag" printable
- "Brazil Facts" printable

LEADER • **Jesus was born to be God's promised Savior**. That's what missionaries want people all over the world to know. The Bible teaches us that we should go and tell all people about the Savior. That's why missionaries go to places like Brazil.

Pray for missionaries in Brazil or the missionaries your church supports.

Key passage (5 minutes)

Show the key passage poster. Lead the boys and girls to read together John 1:1-2. Sing the key passage song.

- Key Passage Poster
- "The Word Was God (John 1:1-2)" song

LEADER • Jesus' life as a human started when the Holy Spirit put Jesus in Mary's womb, but God the Son has always existed. Our key passage helps us understand that Jesus—the Word—is God the Son and was with God the Father and God the Holy Spirit all along, even in the very beginning.

Sing (4 minutes)

· "Take It to the Lord" song

LEADER • Jesus completely understands our struggles and gives us the power to love and obey God. He is the best friend we could ever have.

Sing together "Take It to the Lord."

Pray (2 minutes)

Invite kids to pray before dismissing to apply the story.

LEADER • Father, thank You for sending Jesus. We know that we do not deserve Him. Thank You that Jesus humbled Himself to be born as a human and even to die as we deserve to die. Help us honor You and obey You out of love each day. Amen.

Dismiss to apply the story

The Gospel: God's Plan for Me

Ask kids if they have ever heard the word *gospel*. Clarify that the word *gospel* means "good news." It is the message about Christ, the kingdom of God, and salvation. Use the following guide to share the gospel with kids.

God rules. Explain to kids that the Bible tells us God created everything, and He is in charge of everything. Invite a volunteer to read Genesis 1:1 from the Bible. Read Revelation 4:11 or Colossians 1:16-17 aloud and explain what these verses mean.

We sinned. Tell kids that since the time of Adam and Eve, everyone has chosen to disobey God. (Romans 3:23) The Bible calls this sin. Because God is holy, God cannot be around sin. Sin separates us from God and deserves God's punishment of death. (Romans 6:23)

God provided. Choose a child to read John 3:16 aloud. Say that God sent His Son, Jesus, the perfect solution to our sin problem, to rescue us from the punishment we deserve. It's something we, as sinners, could never earn on our own. Jesus alone saves us. Read and explain Ephesians 2:8-9.

Jesus gives. Share with kids that Jesus lived a perfect life, died on the cross for our sins, and rose again. Because Jesus gave up His life for us, we can be welcomed into God's family for eternity. This is the best gift ever! Read Romans 5:8; 2 Corinthians 5:21; or 1 Peter 3:18.

We respond. Tell kids that they can respond to Jesus. Read Romans 10:9-10,13. Review these aspects of our response: Believe in your heart that Jesus alone saves you through what He's already done on the cross. Repent, turning from self and sin to Jesus. Tell God and others that your faith is in Jesus.

Offer to talk with any child who is interested in responding to Jesus. Provide *I'm a Christian Now!* for new Christians to take home and complete with their families.

APPLY the Story

SESSION TITLE: Jesus Was Born
BIBLE PASSAGE: Luke 2
STORY POINT: Jesus was born to be God's promised Savior.
KEY PASSAGE: John 1:1-2
BIG PICTURE QUESTION: Is Jesus God or a human? As the Son of God, Jesus is both fully God and fully human.

Key passage activity (5 minutes)

· Key Passage Poster

Lead the kids to say the key passage with you a few times. Then cover or hide any posters displaying the verses and say them again, skipping a single word and replacing it with a clap. Ask the kids which word you skipped. Then say the passage and replace two words with claps. Provide an opportunity for kids to supply the missing words. Continue in this way until you clap the entire key passage and kids say it from memory.

SAY • Our key passage comes from the Book of John. John explained that the Word was with God and was God. This helps us understand that Jesus is God the Son, and He has always existed with God the Father. Even though Jesus' life as a human had a definite beginning, Jesus has no beginning and no end.

Discussion & Bible skills (10 minutes)

· Bibles, 1 per kid
· Story Point Poster
· Small Group Timeline and Map Set
   (005802970, optional)

Distribute a Bible to each kid. Help kids find Luke 2. Ask the kids which division Luke is in. (*New Testament, Gospels*) Ask them to name the other three books in this division. (*Matthew, Mark, John*) Remind the kids that the Gospels tell of Jesus' life, death, and resurrection.

Ask the following questions. Lead the group to discuss:

Option: Retell or review the Bible story using the bolded text of the Bible story script.

1. Why did Mary and Joseph travel to Bethlehem? (*to be registered in the census, Luke 2:1-5*)
2. Why was Jesus laid in a manger? (*There was no guest room available, Luke 2:7*)
3. Who were Jesus' first visitors? (*shepherds, Luke 2:8,16*)
4. Why is Jesus' birth so incredible? *Guide kids to discuss both the unusual circumstances of Jesus' arrival—such as the angel choirs proclaiming His birth—and the miraculous nature of Jesus' full divinity being wrapped in full humanity. Remind kids that Jesus the Messiah had been promised to come for thousands of years, and God is faithful.*
5. Why is it important that Jesus came as a human baby? *Help kids understand that God's plan to destroy sin required a perfect sacrifice. Jesus' birth as a human meant that He could grow up and lay down His life for us. He could live the perfect human life we are unable to live and die the kind of death we deserve. Jesus' full humanity is why He could die to save humans.*
6. Why is it important that Jesus remained God? *Explain that Jesus' nature as fully God is what allowed Him to bear the weight of God's punishment for sin in a human body. The complete power of God in Jesus also gave Him the power to reject temptation and live a perfectly sinless life.*

SAY • **Jesus was born to be God's promised Savior**. He was born fully human and did not stop being fully God. Jesus is the only Savior; no one is like Him. Jesus grew up, never sinned, and died for our sin. On the third day, He rose again to defeat sin and death.

Activity choice (10 minutes)

 OPTION 1: Beaded jewelry

· various beads
· colored string or yarn
· scissors

Tip: Use this activity option to reinforce the missions moment found in Teach the Story.

Invite kids to make beaded bracelets or necklaces. Cut a length of string or yarn for each kid, about 5 inches for a bracelet, or 12 for a necklace. Let kids choose from a variety of beads to make their own pattern or design. Direct them to string their beads. Help them tie knots to finish the necklaces and bracelets.

Encourage kids to give the jewelry they made to others and tell those people about Jesus. If possible, allow them to make a second piece of jewelry to keep. As they work, remind them of missionaries in Brazil who tell artists and craftsmen about Jesus.

SAY • Arts and crafts are very popular in Brazil. Many artists enjoy painting, making things out of clay, weaving baskets, and making colorful jewelry. Beaded jewelry is common and is often sold in markets. A great way to live on mission is to use your artistic talents to glorify God and tell others about Jesus. You can do that right in your own hometown, too!

LOW PREP

· stopwatch

OPTION 2: The minute game

Gather the kids together and instruct them to stand up. Challenge them to sit down when they think exactly one minute has elapsed. Use a stopwatch and keep track of who sits closest to a minute without going over. Play additional rounds using different lengths of time.

SAY • In that game, we didn't know exactly when a minute would be up, but we had the ability to count seconds to try and come close. Waiting for something can be especially hard if you don't know when it will happen.

Imagine God's people, who had been waiting for thousands of years. They did not know exactly when the Messiah would come, but they knew God would be faithful. When Jesus was born, it was somewhat unexpected. If it hadn't been for the angels proclaiming the news to shepherds, only Mary and Joseph would have even known the Messiah was there! But all that waiting was worth it when **Jesus was born to be God's promised Savior.**

Reflection and prayer (5 minutes)

Distribute a sheet of paper to each child. Ask the kids to write about or draw a picture to answer the following questions:

- What does this story teach me about God or about the gospel?
- What does this story teach me about myself?
- Whom can I tell about this story?

Make sure to send the sheets home with kids alongside the activity page so that parents can see what their kids have been learning.

If time remains, take prayer requests or allow kids to complete the Bible story coloring page provided with this session. Pray for your group.

· pencils and crayons
· paper
· Bible Story Coloring Page, 1 per kid

Tip: Give parents this week's *Big Picture Cards for Families* to allow families to interact with the biblical content at home.

Unit 19 · Session 4
Jesus Was Dedicated

BIBLE PASSAGE:
Luke 2

STORY POINT:
Simeon and Anna worshiped
Jesus as the Messiah.

KEY PASSAGE:
John 1:1-2

BIG PICTURE QUESTION:
Is Jesus God or a human? As
the Son of God, Jesus is both
fully God and fully human.

INTRODUCE THE STORY
(10–15 MINUTES)
PAGE 54

→

TEACH THE STORY
(25–30 MINUTES)
PAGE 56

→

APPLY THE STORY
(25–30 MINUTES)
PAGE 62

Additional resources are available at gospelproject.com. For free training and
session-by-session help, visit Ministrygrid.com/thegospelproject.

LEADER Bible Study

God had chosen Mary and Joseph to be Jesus' earthly parents. Mary and Joseph named their baby Jesus, obeying God in faith that salvation had indeed come into the world. (See Matt. 1:21.) When the time came for Jesus to be dedicated and Mary to be purified, Mary and Joseph took Jesus to the temple in Jerusalem.

According to the law given to Moses, after a woman gave birth, she was "unclean" and would observe a period of purification. Then she would bring an offering to the priest. (See Lev. 12:1-6.) Jesus was about five weeks old when Mary and Joseph dedicated Him to the Lord and offered the required sacrifice.

Simeon was also at the temple that day, not by mere coincidence but by the Holy Spirit's leading. (Luke 2:27) Simeon spent His life serving the Lord and looked forward to the day when God would keep His promise to comfort Israel. (See Isa. 57:18.) God promised that Simeon would live long enough to see the Messiah. That day had finally come. Imagine his joy. At last, the Savior was here!

4

Simeon saw the baby Jesus, took Him in his arms, and praised God. Simeon expressed prophetic praise, trusting by faith that God would keep His promise through this child: "My eyes have seen your salvation" (Luke 2:30). Through Jesus, everyone would be able to see God's plan. Jesus would be a light for all the nations. He would bring honor to Israel.

Anna, a prophetess, also praised too. At well over a hundred years old, Anna began to speak about Jesus to everyone who was looking forward to God's bringing salvation to His people.

Today, we can have faith in Jesus and His finished work on the cross for our salvation. When God opens our eyes to the good news of the gospel, we can live and die in peace, for our eyes have seen His salvation. We can joyfully share this good news with others.

The BIBLE Story

Jesus Was Dedicated

Luke 2

Mary and Joseph's baby—God's own Son—was a few days old when Mary and Joseph named Him Jesus, just like the angel had told them to do. **One day, when Jesus was a few weeks old, Mary and Joseph took Jesus to the temple in Jerusalem.**

Mary and Joseph wanted to obey God and His law. The law that God gave Moses said, "When a woman's first son is born, his parents must dedicate him to the Lord." The law also said that the child's parents should give a sacrifice. **At the temple, Mary and Joseph presented Jesus to the Lord and offered two birds as a sacrifice.**

Another man was at the temple. His name was Simeon. Simeon loved God, and He trusted in God's promise to send a Messiah to save people from sin. **God's Spirit was with Simeon, and God had told Simeon that he would not die until he saw the One who would rescue people from their sin.**

That day, God's Spirit had led Simeon to the temple. **Simeon saw Jesus and picked Him up in his arms.** God's Spirit showed Simeon that Jesus was the promised Messiah. Simeon was so happy. He praised God and said, "Lord, you can let me die now. You kept Your promise, and I have seen the One who will save people from sin." **Simeon said that Jesus would save God's people, the Israelites, and Jesus would also save people from other nations.**

Mary and Joseph were amazed at what Simeon said. Simeon blessed Mary and Joseph. He told Mary that being Jesus' mother would be a very good thing, but it would also be very hard. Some people would love Jesus, but others would hate Him. Things were going to happen that would make Mary very sad.

A woman named Anna was at the temple too. Anna's husband had died, and Anna was very old. She stayed at the temple and worshiped God all the time. **Anna came up to Simeon, Jesus, Mary, and Joseph and she began to thank God. Anna talked about Jesus to people who were waiting for God to keep His promise to send a Savior. She told them the good news: the Savior was here!**

Mary and Joseph finished dedicating Jesus and making sacrifices to God. They obeyed God's law. Then they went back home to Nazareth. **Jesus grew up and was strong and healthy. He was wise, and God was happy with Him.**

Christ Connection: Throughout the Old Testament, God promised the arrival of a king who would redeem people. When Jesus arrived, Simeon and Anna knew He was the promised Messiah. Today, we have faith that Jesus is God's Son. We can trust Jesus for our salvation, and like Simeon and Anna, we should share the good news.

Bible Storytelling Tips

- **Act it out:** Choose four volunteers to silently act out the story as you tell it. Provide a baby doll as the baby Jesus.
- **Use hand gestures:** Capture kids' attention by moving your hands as you tell the story. Raise them as Simeon speaks or hold them to your head like Jesus' amazed parents.

INTRODUCE the Story

SESSION TITLE: Jesus Was Dedicated
BIBLE PASSAGE: Luke 2
STORY POINT: Simeon and Anna worshiped Jesus as the Messiah.
KEY PASSAGE: John 1:1-2
BIG PICTURE QUESTION: Is Jesus God or a human? As the Son of God, Jesus is both fully God and fully human.

Welcome time

Greet each kid as he or she arrives. Use this time to collect the offering, fill out attendance sheets, and help new kids connect to your group. Prompt kids to discuss things they really want to do someday. When will they do those things?

SAY • We often have things we want to see or do in our lives. In our story today, we will learn about two people who finally got to experience something they had hoped to for many years. How do you think you would feel?

Activity page (5 minutes)

- "Waiting for Whom?" activity page, 1 per kid
- pencils or markers

Invite kids to complete the "Waiting for Whom?" activity page. Kids will find the letters scattered in the picture and unscramble them to reveal the words *Jesus Messiah*. If kids get stuck, remind them that the letters are color-coded with the blanks they can go in.

SAY • God had promised to send the Messiah, and now that Jesus was in the world, that promise was fulfilled. Today we will learn about two people specifically who had been waiting to meet the Messiah. How do you feel when you are waiting for things?

Session starter (10 minutes)

OPTION 1: Jesus is …

Instruct the kids to sit in a circle. Ask each kid to say a word that describes Jesus. Tell the kids not to say the same word as someone else. Be ready to help kids who get stuck or who had a word in mind when someone else said it first. For an added twist, challenge the kids to work their way through the alphabet, providing a word that starts with each letter.

SAY • Those were some great things to say about Jesus. Jesus is God the Son, and He is perfect and wonderful. He is our Savior and King. Today we will hear a story about a time Mary and Joseph heard some incredible things about their baby boy from two people who had just recently met Him!

OPTION 2: How long?

Give each kid three or four index cards and a pencil. Provide scenarios and instruct the kids to write down how long they would wait in the scenario. Then help the kids line up in order by how long they would wait. Play additional rounds as time allows.

· index cards, 3 or 4 per kid
· pencils

Suggested scenarios:
  • You are in line for the best roller coaster.
  • You are waiting for tickets to a cool new movie.
  • You are waiting for a dance recital to begin.

SAY • We don't all agree on what is worth waiting for, but today we will learn about two people who knew they were waiting on something spectacular. What do you think they were waiting for?

Transition to teach the story

TEACH the Story

SESSION TITLE: Jesus Was Dedicated
BIBLE PASSAGE: Luke 2
STORY POINT: Simeon and Anna worshiped Jesus as the Messiah.
KEY PASSAGE: John 1:1-2
BIG PICTURE QUESTION: Is Jesus God or a human? As the Son of God, Jesus is both fully God and fully human.

Countdown

· countdown video

Show the countdown video as you transition to teach the story. Set it to end as the session begins.

Introduce the session (3 minutes)

· leader attire
· camera on a strap

[Leader enters wearing casual clothing and carrying a camera on a strap.]

Tip: If you prefer not to use themed content or characters, adapt or omit this introduction.

LEADER • Holy moly! You all won't believe what was just announced in *Photography Semi-Quarterly* magazine. A special new model of a camera is going to be released soon. It's going to have the most powerful optical zoom lens ever invented and a special infrared flash to make night-vision photos easier than ever. Basically, anyone who takes photography seriously will be eagerly waiting for this puppy to drop. It's got a hefty price tag, so I'm going to start saving up for it so I can buy it as soon as it goes on sale. I wonder if they might publish a semi-quarter-off coupon in the magazine. I wonder how much off that would actually be.

Anyway, I wanted to share that exciting news. I suppose for many of you that may not seem very exciting, but for photography enthusiasts it will be worth the wait. You know, that makes me think of a Bible story where two people experienced something that was definitely worth the wait. Let me tell you about it.

Big picture question (1 minute)

LEADER • Part of the story will make more sense if we remember our big picture question and answer. Can anyone say it for us? [*Allow responses.*] Great job! *Is Jesus God or a human? As the Son of God, Jesus is both fully God and fully human*. This means that Jesus completely understands what it feels like to be human. He can relate to our fears, our frustrations, the ways we are tempted, and our pain and sadness. Jesus also has all the power and glory of God. He is God the Son and was able to bear on the cross the full weight of God's anger toward sin.

Giant timeline (1 minute)

Show the giant timeline. Point to individual Bible stories as you review.

· Giant Timeline

LEADER • Jesus had an earthly family, just as we do. **Jesus' family line proved He is the Messiah**. Jesus is the fulfillment of all God's promises to Adam, Abraham, David, and more. Then we learned that God sent a messenger to go before Jesus just as He promised He would. **John was born to prepare the way for Jesus**. Last week, we finally got to the moment God's people had been waiting for: **Jesus was born to be God's promised Savior**. This week, we'll learn about the time Jesus was dedicated in the temple.

Tell the Bible story (10 minutes)

- Bibles
- "Jesus Was Dedicated" video
- Big Picture Question Poster
- Bible Story Picture Poster
- Story Point Poster

Open your Bible to Luke 2. Use the Bible storytelling tips on the Bible story page to help you tell the story, or show the Bible story video "Jesus Was Dedicated."

LEADER • One thing I want to point out is that Mary and Joseph obeyed the laws God had given His people about how to present a baby at the temple. Jesus' parents knew Jesus was God's Son and were committed to raising Him the way God said to raise children. Jesus' whole life perfectly fulfilled God's laws, even when He was just a baby!

It's also interesting to see that Simeon found Jesus in the temple because God's Spirit led him there. God told Simeon that he would live to see the day the Messiah arrived, and God is always faithful. Simeon praised God and declared the truth about Jesus: He would save people from sin. The nation of Israel had been waiting for years and years to see the Messiah, but not everyone lived to meet Him. What a special feeling that must have been for Simeon.

After Anna met Jesus, she began to tell those around her about Jesus. She understood God's faithfulness too. The people had been waiting for salvation, and the One who would provide it had finally arrived. **Simeon and Anna worshiped Jesus as the Messiah**.

Note: You may use this opportunity to use Scripture and the guide provided to explain how to become a Christian. Make sure kids know when and where they can ask questions.

Christ connection

LEADER • Simeon and Anna did not just understand who Jesus is; they told others about Him and what He would do. Throughout the Old Testament, God promised the arrival of a King who would redeem people. When Jesus arrived, Simeon and Anna knew He was the promised Messiah. Today, we have faith that Jesus is God's Son. We can trust Jesus for our salvation, and like Simeon and Anna, we should share the good news.

Questions from kids video (3 minutes)

Show the "Unit 19, Session 4" questions from kids video. Prompt kids to think about how we will know when Jesus returns to earth. Guide them to discuss what they think it will be like.

· "Unit 19, Session 4" Questions from Kids video

Missions moment (3 minutes)

Play the "Relentless Love (Part 2)" missions video.

LEADER • We have been learning about missionaries in Brazil. In a previous video, we met missionaries Brandi and Amanda. They want people in Brazil to know Jesus personally and to worship Him, like **Simeon and Anna worshiped Jesus as the Messiah**. Brandi and Amanda led another woman named Amanda to Jesus, and now God can use her to share the good news with even more people!

Pray for Amanda, other new believers in Brazil, and the missionaries your church supports.

· "Relentless Love (Part 2)" missions video

Key passage (5 minutes)

Show the key passage poster. Lead the boys and girls to read together John 1:1-2. Then sing the key passage song.

LEADER • John began his book with this key passage. His writing, inspired by God, helps us understand Jesus' nature. Jesus has always existed. Even though His life as a human had a starting point, God the Son has

· Key Passage Poster
· "The Word Was God (John 1:1-2)" song

no beginning and no end. At the start of creation, Jesus was already there. He was with God the Father and God the Spirit then, and He is eternally God the Son.

Sing (4 minutes)

· "Jesus Messiah" song

LEADER • Jesus was no ordinary baby. Anna and Simeon understood who Jesus is and told others about Him. He is the Messiah. Let's sing praises to Him.

Sing together "Jesus Messiah."

Pray (2 minutes)

Invite kids to pray before dismissing to apply the story.

LEADER • Lord, You are good and Your mercy goes on forever. We praise You alone because of who You are and what You have done. Help us trust You daily. Make our obedience an overflow of our love for You. Thank You for sending Jesus the Messiah to save us. Amen.

Dismiss to apply the story

The Gospel: God's Plan for Me

Ask kids if they have ever heard the word *gospel*. Clarify that the word *gospel* means "good news." It is the message about Christ, the kingdom of God, and salvation. Use the following guide to share the gospel with kids.

God rules. Explain to kids that the Bible tells us God created everything, and He is in charge of everything. Invite a volunteer to read Genesis 1:1 from the Bible. Read Revelation 4:11 or Colossians 1:16-17 aloud and explain what these verses mean.

We sinned. Tell kids that since the time of Adam and Eve, everyone has chosen to disobey God. (Romans 3:23) The Bible calls this sin. Because God is holy, God cannot be around sin. Sin separates us from God and deserves God's punishment of death. (Romans 6:23)

God provided. Choose a child to read John 3:16 aloud. Say that God sent His Son, Jesus, the perfect solution to our sin problem, to rescue us from the punishment we deserve. It's something we, as sinners, could never earn on our own. Jesus alone saves us. Read and explain Ephesians 2:8-9.

Jesus gives. Share with kids that Jesus lived a perfect life, died on the cross for our sins, and rose again. Because Jesus gave up His life for us, we can be welcomed into God's family for eternity. This is the best gift ever! Read Romans 5:8; 2 Corinthians 5:21; or 1 Peter 3:18.

We respond. Tell kids that they can respond to Jesus. Read Romans 10:9-10,13. Review these aspects of our response: Believe in your heart that Jesus alone saves you through what He's already done on the cross. Repent, turning from self and sin to Jesus. Tell God and others that your faith is in Jesus.

Offer to talk with any child who is interested in responding to Jesus. Provide *I'm a Christian Now!* for new Christians to take home and complete with their families.

APPLY the Story

SESSION TITLE: Jesus Was Dedicated
BIBLE PASSAGE: Luke 2
STORY POINT: Simeon and Anna worshiped Jesus as the Messiah.
KEY PASSAGE: John 1:1-2
BIG PICTURE QUESTION: Is Jesus God or a human? As the Son of God, Jesus is both fully God and fully human.

Key passage activity (5 minutes)

· Key Passage Poster

Break the key passage into a few phrases. Teach the kids a call and response chant where you say a phrase and they say it back to you. Work your way through the entire key passage in this way, then select a volunteer to lead the call and response without your help. Repeat this process as time allows, selecting new kids to lead each time.

SAY • Jesus' life as a human started when Mary became pregnant, but God the Son existed long before that. In fact, He has no beginning and no end. He has always existed and will always exist. That is what our key passage teaches. Jesus was with God the Father and the Holy Spirit at the start of creation, and He is God the Son.

Discussion & Bible skills (10 minutes)

· Bibles, 1 per kid
· Story Point Poster
· Small Group Timeline and Map Set
  (005802970, optional)

Distribute a Bible to each kid. Help kids find Luke 2. Consider using the New Testament Israel Map to show the location of Jerusalem. Explain that the temple, where today's Bible story was set, would have been in Jerusalem. Remind the kids that the Gospels division contains four accounts of Jesus' life, ministry, death, and resurrection.

Ask the following questions. Lead the group to discuss:

Option: Retell or review the Bible story using the bolded text of the Bible story script.

1. Why did Mary and Joseph bring Jesus to the temple as a baby? (*to dedicate Him according to God's law, Luke 2:22-23*)

2. Why did Simeon say "You can let me die now"? (*Simeon had seen God fulfill His promise to send the Messiah, Luke 2:29-32*)

3. Whom did Anna tell about Jesus? (*those who had been waiting on the Lord's salvation, Luke 2:38*)

4. How would Jesus provide salvation? *Guide kids to think about Jesus' death on the cross. Remind the kids that the fair payment of sin is death and that Jesus died in our place. He took on the punishment of God's anger toward sin and died. Then He rose again to prove His sacrifice was enough.*

5. What are ways people must respond to Jesus? *Discuss the reactions of Simeon and Anna, who were excited and happy and told others about Jesus. Then discuss why some people might not believe the good news, or might feel it is too good (or they are too bad) to accept the gospel as true. Point out that some people might think they know Jesus but never have a real relationship with Him.*

6. What other promises has God given us? *Remind kids that God has promised salvation to everyone who trusts in Jesus. He has promised to send Jesus back to fix everything sin has broken. He has promised to give us new life, joy, and peace through Jesus. Help kids understand that He has not promised an easy life.*

SAY • **Simeon and Anna worshiped Jesus as the Messiah.** Jesus is the Messiah, and we can worship Him too.

Activity choice (10 minutes)

· "Missionaries Who
 Travel" printable
· scissors
· luggage, 3 differently
 sized pieces

OPTION 1: To the ends of the earth

Print and cut apart the "Missionaries Who Travel" printable. Place each missionary description in a piece of luggage that corresponds to the length of travel described. For example, place the description of a volunteer missionary in the smallest bag, the description of a short-term missionary in the medium bag, and the description of the career missionary in the largest bag.

Tip: Use this
activity option
to reinforce the
missions moment
found in Teach the
Story.

SAY • At some point, God may call you to travel to another place to be a missionary. You might go for just a few days or weeks. Maybe you will spend a few months or a year in another country. Or perhaps you will move with your family to a new home where you will tell people about Jesus for many years to come. No matter where God tells you to go, you can be part of telling others the good news of Jesus so they can worship Him as the Messiah.

LOW PREP

· paper
· pencils
· Bibles (optional)

OPTION 2: Praise songs

Form groups of about five kids. Provide each group with a sheet of paper and pencil. You may pass out Bibles and help kids find Luke 2:29-32. Encourage the kids to work in their groups to write songs praising Jesus as the Messiah. Be prepared to help them rhyme words, or suggest popular tunes their songs could be sung to. Allow each group a chance to sing their song for the rest of the groups.

SAY • Wow, those were some great new songs. Worshiping Jesus is one of the most worthwhile things we can do. Jesus is our perfect Savior. He is our Creator and King. We can worship Him by loving others, obeying Him, or giving Him the glory in our lives. We can also sing these songs we've written. **Simeon and Anna worshiped Jesus as the Messiah**. Who can you teach your song to help them worship Jesus too?

Reflection and prayer (5 minutes)

Distribute a sheet of paper to each child. Ask the kids to write about or draw a picture to answer the following questions:

- What does this story teach me about God or about the gospel?
- What does this story teach me about myself?
- Whom can I tell about this story?

Make sure to send the sheets home with kids alongside the activity page so that parents can see what their kids have been learning.

If time remains, take prayer requests or allow kids to complete the Bible story coloring page provided with this session. Pray for your group.

· pencils and crayons
· paper
· Bible Story Coloring Page, 1 per kid

Tip: Give parents this week's *Big Picture Cards for Families* to allow families to interact with the biblical content at home.

Unit 19 • Session 5
Jesus as a Child

BIBLE PASSAGE:
Matthew 2; Luke 2

STORY POINT:
Even as a child, Jesus wanted
to do His Father's plan.

KEY PASSAGE:
John 1:1-2

BIG PICTURE QUESTION:
Is Jesus God or a human? As
the Son of God, Jesus is both
fully God and fully human.

INTRODUCE THE STORY	TEACH THE STORY	APPLY THE STORY
(10–15 MINUTES)	(25–30 MINUTES)	(25–30 MINUTES)
PAGE 70	PAGE 72	PAGE 78

 → →

Additional resources are available at gospelproject.com. For free training and
session-by-session help, visit Ministrygrid.com/thegospelproject.

LEADER Bible Study

The Gospel of Luke records just two narratives about Jesus' childhood: His dedication (Luke 2:21-40) and His visit to the temple when He was 12 years old (Luke 2:41-52). The Gospel of Matthew includes another story: a visit from some wise men. These stories of Jesus as a child set the stage for Jesus' ministry as an adult.

After Jesus was born, God put a star in the sky as a sign. Wise men from the east followed the star to Jerusalem, looking for a new king. They found Jesus, who was probably 1 or 2 years old, in Bethlehem and they worshiped Him as King. Later, Jesus and His family settled in Nazareth, where Jesus grew up.

In Bible times, a Jewish boy became a man at 13. His father would train him to take on all the responsibilities of adulthood—social and spiritual. Joseph was a carpenter, and he likely trained Jesus in his trade. When Mary and Joseph went to Jerusalem to celebrate Passover, Joseph might have taken Jesus, who was about 12, around the city to teach Him the significance of the temple and to explain the purpose of the Passover feast.

Jesus' parents headed home after the feast. They assumed Jesus was among their traveling companions, but He wasn't. Jesus had stayed behind at the temple. A full day passed before Mary and Joseph noticed Jesus was missing. They hurried back to Jerusalem and finally found Him at the temple. Jesus asked His mother, "Didn't you know that I had to be in My Father's house?" Mary and Joseph did not understand. But Jesus is God's Son, and it was necessary that He honor His true Father. In all this, Jesus did not sin.

The Bible does not give many details about Jesus' childhood, but we know that as Jesus got older, He grew "in wisdom and stature, and in favor with God and with people" (Luke 2:52). Jesus carried out God's plan to reconcile the world to Himself. (2 Cor. 5:19)

5

The **BIBLE** Story

Jesus as a Child
Matthew 2; Luke 2

After Jesus was born, wise men followed a star to Bethlehem to find the new king of the Jews. The wise men worshiped Jesus as King. When they left, an angel told Joseph in a dream to leave Bethlehem because King Herod wanted to kill Jesus. So **Mary, Joseph, and Jesus** went to Egypt until Herod died. Then they **went back to** Israel and lived in **Nazareth. Jesus grew up in Nazareth.**

Every year, Jesus' parents traveled to Jerusalem for the Passover feast. Passover was the biggest holiday for the Jewish people. Many people traveled to Jerusalem to celebrate and remember when God saved His people from slavery in Egypt.

When Jesus was 12 years old, Jesus and His family went to Jerusalem together. When it was time to go home, Mary and Joseph began traveling to Nazareth with a large group of people. They didn't notice that Jesus was not with them; they thought He was among the group of travelers. But Jesus was not with the group. He **had stayed behind in Jerusalem.**

Mary and Joseph had been walking for a whole day when they started to look for Jesus. They looked among their relatives and friends, but they could not find Him. So Mary and Joseph **went back to Jerusalem. They searched everywhere for Jesus.** The city was so big, and Jesus was just a boy.

Finally, they found Him at the temple. Jesus was listening to the teachers and asking them questions. Everyone who heard Jesus could hardly believe how much Jesus understood. When Jesus' parents saw Him, they were surprised. Mary said, "Son, why have You done this? Your father and I were worried. We've been looking everywhere for You."

"Why were you looking for Me?" Jesus asked. "Didn't you know that I had to be in My Father's house?" But Mary and Joseph did not understand what Jesus was talking about. **Then Jesus went back to Nazareth with Mary and Joseph. Jesus was always obedient to them**, and Mary remembered all of these things.

As Jesus grew up, He became even wiser. God was pleased with Him, and so was everyone who knew Him.

Christ Connection: God sent Jesus to earth with a purpose. Even as a child, Jesus wanted to honor God. God blessed Jesus as He got ready to follow His Father's plan: to die on the cross and rescue people from sin.

Bible Storytelling Tips

• **Change positions:** Move around the room as you describe Mary and Joseph's journey.
• **Use facial expressions:** Reflect emotions of the story when Jesus was missing and when He was found.

INTRODUCE the Story

SESSION TITLE: Jesus as a Child
BIBLE PASSAGE: Matthew 2; Luke 2
STORY POINT: Even as a child, Jesus wanted to do His Father's plan.
KEY PASSAGE: John 1:1-2
BIG PICTURE QUESTION: Is Jesus God or a human? As the Son of God, Jesus is both fully God and fully human.

Welcome time

Greet each kid as he or she arrives. Use this time to collect the offering, fill out attendance sheets, and help new kids connect to your group. Prompt kids to discuss things they have learned to do and things they want to learn to do.

SAY • When we are born, we are basically helpless, and we must rely on others to take care of us. As we grow up, we learn many different skills and lots of information. Today, we will learn about a time after Jesus was a baby, but before He was all grown up. We will see that people were surprised by how much He understood despite His being a child.

Activity page (5 minutes)

· "Giving Treasure"
activity page,
1 per kid
· pencils or markers

Invite kids to complete the "Giving Treasure" activity page. Kids will use the space provided to draw a picture of something they treasure that they could give to Jesus to worship Him.

SAY • Those are some great treasures you all drew. Today we will hear about a time when wise men visited Jesus and brought Him treasures to worship Him.

Session starter (10 minutes)

OPTION 1: Find the star

Hide a star-shaped paper cutout somewhere in the room. Invite the kids to find the star and bring it to you. For a competitive twist, hide multiple stars and see who can find the most in a given time limit.

- star-shaped paper cutout, 1 or more
- timer (optional)

SAY • The wise men who visited Jesus followed a bright star. When they found Jesus in Bethlehem, they presented Him with gold, frankincense, and myrrh—three valuable treasures. Jesus was no ordinary child, and His extraordinary nature would become more and more clear as He grew up. We'll learn more about it today.

OPTION 2: Tough questions

LOW PREP

Invite the kids to come up with appropriate, silly questions to ask a child volunteer. The volunteer must attempt to answer the question without laughing or smiling. She may make up the answers, and the answers do not have to be accurate. Whoever makes her laugh gets to answer questions in the next round. Play as time allows.

SAY • Those questions were pretty silly. Sometimes though, we face real questions that are difficult to answer because they require more wisdom than we might have. Today we will learn about a time Jesus proved He understood difficult questions and had lots of wise answers, even while He was just a boy.

Transition to teach the story

TEACH the Story

SESSION TITLE: Jesus as a Child
BIBLE PASSAGE: Matthew 2; Luke 2
STORY POINT: Even as a child, Jesus wanted to do His Father's plan.
KEY PASSAGE: John 1:1-2
BIG PICTURE QUESTION: Is Jesus God or a human? As the Son of God, Jesus is both fully God and fully human.

Countdown

· countdown video

Show the countdown video as you transition to teach the story. Set it to end as the session begins.

Introduce the session (3 minutes)

· leader attire
· camera on a strap

[Leader enters wearing casual clothing and carrying a camera on a strap.]

Tip: If you prefer not to use themed content or characters, adapt or omit this introduction.

LEADER • Hey, kids! Welcome to my photography studio. You know, a large percentage of the photo shoots I do are kids' portraits. Parents love to have pictures of their children as they grow up. It can be lots of fun to look back on how we used to look or what we used to be interested in.

One day, each of you will be an adult, and chances are, the adults in your life now will say things like "I can't believe how grown up you are!" or "where has the time gone?" By getting pictures of you now, your parents, grandparents, or teachers can hold onto their memories of you as a child a bit more clearly.

You know, that reminds me of a Bible story. The Bible doesn't contain a lot of information about Jesus as a child, but there are a few stories. The Bible even tells us that Jesus' mother held onto these memories of Jesus as a child and treasured them in her heart!

Big picture question (1 minute)

LEADER • Remember, Jesus had an earthly mother—Mary—and Joseph raised Jesus as his own son. But Jesus is really God's Son. That brings us to our big picture question and answer. *Is Jesus God or a human? As the Son of God, Jesus is both fully God and fully human.* Jesus understands our pain, sadness, and brokenness that come from sin, but He never sinned. He carried God's punishment for sin. Only Jesus could do both those things; only Jesus is fully God and human.

Giant timeline (1 minute)

Show the giant timeline. Point to individual Bible stories as you review.

· Giant Timeline

LEADER • A few weeks back, we talked about Jesus' family. We learned that **Jesus' family line proved He is the Messiah**. Later we learned that **John was born to prepare the way for Jesus**, and **Jesus was born to be God's promised Savior**. When Jesus was dedicated at the temple according to God's law, **Simeon and Anna worshiped Jesus as the Messiah**. This week, we will hear about something else from Jesus' childhood.

· Bibles
· "Jesus as a Child" video
· Big Picture Question Poster
· Bible Story Picture Poster
· Story Point Poster

Tell the Bible story (10 minutes)

Open your Bible to Matthew 2; Luke 2. Use the Bible storytelling tips on the Bible story page to help you tell the story, or show the Bible story video "Jesus as a Child."

LEADER • In any other circumstances, a mom and dad would probably be very worried if strangers showed up at their door with presents for their child. But Jesus was not an ordinary child. The wise men understood who He was and offered great treasures to worship Him. And we see more clearly who Jesus is from the next part of the story.

Some of you may have had scary situations where you got separated from your parents in a crowded place. It can feel terrifying—especially for a parent. Imagine how Mary and Joseph might have felt. God had given them the important job of raising the Messiah, and they left Jerusalem without Him!

But remember, Jesus was no ordinary child. While you or I might have been afraid or gotten ourselves into trouble without parents around, Jesus was in the temple discussing God with the teachers of the law! The Bible tells us that everyone there was amazed by Jesus' ability to understand the Scriptures.

Even as a child, Jesus wanted to do His Father's plan. He understood all along that He would glorify God by obeying God's plans.

Christ connection

Note: You may use this opportunity to use Scripture and the guide provided to explain how to become a Christian. Make sure kids know when and where they can ask questions.

LEADER • God sent Jesus to earth with a purpose. Even as a child, Jesus wanted to honor God. God blessed Jesus as He got ready to follow His Father's plan: to die on the cross and rescue people from sin. When we trust in Jesus, God forgives our sin and makes us part of His family. When we trust God, He will use us in amazing ways to spread the good news. That is His plan for believers, and we can all be a part of it.

Questions from kids video (3 minutes)

Show the "Unit 19, Session 5" questions from kids video. Prompt kids to think about God's plans for them. Guide them to discuss how they can confidently tell others about Jesus and what He's done for them.

· "Unit 19, Session 5" Questions from Kids video

Missions moment (3 minutes)

Display the "Photos from Brazil" printable and ask a volunteer to read each caption. Ask the kids what they think it means for Christians to follow God's plan on mission in Brazil, or anywhere we go. Allow time for kids to discuss.

· "Photos from Brazil" printable

LEADER • **Even as a child, Jesus wanted to do His Father's plan**. Though you are young, you can follow God's plan and be on mission wherever you go! We live on mission by loving other people the way God loves us and by telling them about the forgiveness we can have through Jesus.

Key passage (5 minutes)

Show the key passage poster. Lead the boys and girls to read together John 1:1-2. Then sing the key passage song.

· Key Passage Poster
· "The Word Was God (John 1:1-2)" song

LEADER • Our key passage reminds us that Jesus—the Word—has always existed. In the beginning, He was there with God the Father. He is God the Son and will continue to exist for eternity.

Sing (4 minutes)

· "Take It to the Lord" song

LEADER • **Even as a child, Jesus wanted to do His Father's plan**, which was to die to save us. Scripture tells us that there's no better friend than that.

Sing together "Take It to the Lord."

Pray (2 minutes)

Invite kids to pray before dismissing to apply the story.

LEADER • Father, thank You for sending Your Son. Thank You that He wanted to obey Your plan to rescue us all along. We know that He is the best friend we could ever have. Help us love and obey You. Amen.

Dismiss to apply the story

The Gospel: God's Plan for Me

Ask kids if they have ever heard the word *gospel*. Clarify that the word *gospel* means "good news." It is the message about Christ, the kingdom of God, and salvation. Use the following guide to share the gospel with kids.

God rules. Explain to kids that the Bible tells us God created everything, and He is in charge of everything. Invite a volunteer to read Genesis 1:1 from the Bible. Read Revelation 4:11 or Colossians 1:16-17 aloud and explain what these verses mean.

We sinned. Tell kids that since the time of Adam and Eve, everyone has chosen to disobey God. (Romans 3:23) The Bible calls this sin. Because God is holy, God cannot be around sin. Sin separates us from God and deserves God's punishment of death. (Romans 6:23)

God provided. Choose a child to read John 3:16 aloud. Say that God sent His Son, Jesus, the perfect solution to our sin problem, to rescue us from the punishment we deserve. It's something we, as sinners, could never earn on our own. Jesus alone saves us. Read and explain Ephesians 2:8-9.

Jesus gives. Share with kids that Jesus lived a perfect life, died on the cross for our sins, and rose again. Because Jesus gave up His life for us, we can be welcomed into God's family for eternity. This is the best gift ever! Read Romans 5:8; 2 Corinthians 5:21; or 1 Peter 3:18.

We respond. Tell kids that they can respond to Jesus. Read Romans 10:9-10,13. Review these aspects of our response: Believe in your heart that Jesus alone saves you through what He's already done on the cross. Repent, turning from self and sin to Jesus. Tell God and others that your faith is in Jesus.

Offer to talk with any child who is interested in responding to Jesus. Provide *I'm a Christian Now!* for new Christians to take home and complete with their families.

APPLY the Story

SESSION TITLE: Jesus as a Child
BIBLE PASSAGE: Matthew 2; Luke 2
STORY POINT: Even as a child, Jesus wanted to do His Father's plan.
KEY PASSAGE: John 1:1-2
BIG PICTURE QUESTION: Is Jesus God or a human? As the Son of God, Jesus is both fully God and fully human.

Key passage activity (5 minutes)

· Key Passage Poster

Tip: In some places, this game is known as "Down by the Banks."

Invite volunteers to say the key passage from memory. Praise each kid's efforts and encourage all the kids to continue working to memorize the key passage. Then instruct the kids to sit in a circle. Each kid will place her left hand under the right hand of the kid on her left. Kids will then take turns saying each word of the key passage in order.

As each kid says a word on his turn, he will move his right hand to clap the right hand of the kid on his left. Then that kid will say the next word, and so on around the circle. The kid to the left of the kid who says the last word of the key passage will try to move her hand before he can clap it. If he claps his own hand, she wins. If he claps her hand before she can move it, he wins. Play as time allows or until all kids have the verses memorized.

Discussion & Bible skills (10 minutes)

· Bibles, 1 per kid
· Story Point Poster
· Small Group Timeline and Map Set
  (005802970, optional)

Distribute a Bible to each kid. Help kids find Luke 2. Ask a volunteer to tell which division Luke is in (*New Testament, Gospels*). Ask another volunteer to tell which other books are in that division, and what they tell. (*Matthew, Mark, John; the story of Jesus' life and ministry on earth*)

Ask the following questions. Lead the group to discuss:

Option: Retell or review the Bible story using the bolded text of the Bible story script.

1. Why did Mary and Joseph travel to Jerusalem each year? (*for the Passover, Luke 2:41*)
2. How long did it take Mary and Joseph to find Jesus? (*three days, Luke 2:46*)
3. What about Jesus astounded people? (*His understanding and His answers, Luke 2:46-47*)
4. Why do you think Jesus' understanding and wisdom were so surprising? *Help kids understand that Jesus would have seemed like an ordinary 12-year-old just by looking at Him. Remind kids that Jesus is fully God and fully human. Jesus was able to understand and explain God's Word as One who had studied it for many years, despite His young age.*
5. Why do you think Jesus said it was necessary for Him to be in His Father's house? *Guide kids to understand that Jesus' Father is God. Remind them that Jesus is God the Son, and He knew God's plans for His life: to make the way for sinners to have eternal life. Jesus understood that He would need to rely on God's power to obey Him, and Jesus wanted to obey God always.*
6. How can we live out God's plans for us? *Discuss the idea that God's plan for all believers is for us to glorify Him by loving others, obeying Him out of love, and sharing the gospel throughout the earth. Remind kids that we can live on mission no matter where we are.*

SAY • **Even as a child, Jesus wanted to do His Father's plan**. He perfectly obeyed His earthly parents and all of God's commands, eventually dying for our sin.

Activity choice (10 minutes)

OPTION 1: Live on mission

Work with parents and other ministry leaders to coordinate volunteer efforts so that your group has opportunities to serve your church and community. Consider leading a group of kids to the nursery to clean and disinfect toys or to the church grounds to pick up litter. Plan and run a food drive or challenge your kids to sweep or vacuum the classrooms in your kids ministry area.

SAY • By helping out in simple ways like these, you are a part of God's plan. You are an important part of this church. Everyone in the church can be a part of God's mission by doing things that serve others. Our mission as a church is to lead others to Jesus; so when we serve at church, we are a part of the mission.

OPTION 2: Give yourself

Form teams of about three kids. Provide each team with a roll of wrapping paper and an adhesive gift bow. Challenge the teams to select one kid to wrap. The first team to wrap a kid from head to toe and stick their bow on top wins. You may also alter the game by awarding points for wrapping style or coverage, and declare a winner not based on speed.

SAY • By the end of that game, some of you looked like giant presents that would have been fun to unwrap. In a way though, this isn't as silly as it sounds. We can give ourselves to God by trusting Him in all areas of our lives.

When we allow God to control our time, talents, money, or other treasures, we are giving Him ourselves. He can use us to glorify Himself and lead others to believe in Jesus. It doesn't matter that you

· various cleaning supplies, such as vacuum cleaners, trash bags, or disinfecting wipes (optional)

Tip: Use this activity option to reinforce the missions moment found in Teach the Story.

LOW PREP

· wrapping paper rolls
· adhesive gift bows

are still young either. **Even as a child, Jesus wanted to do His Father's plan.**

Reflection and prayer (5 minutes)

Distribute a sheet of paper to each child. Ask the kids to write about or draw a picture to answer the following questions:

- What does this story teach me about God or about the gospel?
- What does this story teach me about myself?
- Whom can I tell about this story?

Make sure to send the sheets home with kids alongside the activity page so that parents can see what their kids have been learning.

If time remains, take prayer requests or allow kids to complete the Bible story coloring page provided with this session. Pray for your group.

· pencils and crayons
· paper
· Bible Story Coloring
  Page, 1 per kid

Tip: Give parents this week's *Big Picture Cards for Families* to allow families to interact with the biblical content at home.

Use Week of:

Unit 20 · Session 1
Jesus' Baptism

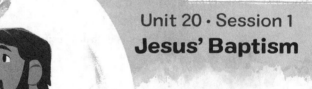

BIBLE PASSAGE:
Matthew 3; Mark 1;
Luke 3; John 1

STORY POINT:
Jesus obeyed God by being baptized.

KEY PASSAGE:
John 3:30

BIG PICTURE QUESTION:
Why did Jesus become human? Jesus
became human to obey His Father's
plan and rescue sinners.

INTRODUCE THE STORY
(10–15 MINUTES)
PAGE 86

→

TEACH THE STORY
(25–30 MINUTES)
PAGE 88

→

APPLY THE STORY
(25–30 MINUTES)
PAGE 94

Additional resources are available at gospelproject.com. For free training and
session-by-session help, visit MinistryGrid.com/thegospelproject.

LEADER Bible Study

Zechariah's son, John, grew up in the wilderness. His ministry began when God's word came to him, and he began preaching near the Jordan River. John worked to get people ready for the coming of Jesus, fulfilling the Old Testament prophecy, "A voice of one crying out: Prepare the way of the LORD in the wilderness" (Isa. 40:3a).

John called people to repent of their sins, and he baptized them in the Jordan River. John also instructed people on right living. (See Luke 3:10-14.) Some of the people suspected that John might be the Messiah, but John insisted, "One who is more powerful than I am is coming" (Luke 3:16).

Before His ministry began, Jesus came from Galilee to be baptized by John at the Jordan River. But John was calling people to a baptism of repentance. Jesus never sinned (see Heb. 4:15; 2 Cor. 5:21), so why did Jesus come to be baptized? John recognized this when he said, "I need to be baptized by you, and yet you come to me?" (Matt. 3:14).

Commentators' ideas vary about why exactly Jesus was baptized. Perhaps He was affirming John's work. Maybe He was identifying with sinners or showing them how they would be saved—through His death, burial, and resurrection. Jesus answered John, "Allow it for now, because this is the way for us to fulfill all righteousness" (Matt. 3:15). Jesus completely obeyed God, and God audibly confirmed His sonship.

As you teach, allow time for kids to ask questions about repentance, salvation, and baptism. Emphasize that baptism is not what saves us; baptism is a way we show that we have been saved. Baptism reminds us that when we trust in Jesus, we die to sin and come into a new way of life—a life lived for Him. (See Rom. 6:3-4.)

The **BIBLE** Story

Jesus' Baptism
Matthew 3; Mark 1; Luke 3; John 1

John the Baptist lived in the wilderness. His clothes were made out of camel's hair and he wore a leather belt around his waist. He ate locusts and wild honey. **John began telling people, "Repent and be baptized because God's kingdom is almost here."**

Some people asked John, "Who are you?" John said, "I am not the Messiah." John also said he wasn't Elijah, and he wasn't the Prophet that God had promised to send after Moses.

"Who are you, then?" they asked.

Long before John was born, the prophet Isaiah said, "Someone is shouting in the wilderness. He says, 'Prepare the way for the Lord; make His paths straight!'" Isaiah was talking about John. John had a very important job. He **was supposed to get people ready for Jesus— God's promised Messiah.**

People started to repent; they turned away from their sins and turned to God for forgiveness. Then John baptized them in the Jordan River. Baptism was a picture that the people's sins had been washed away.

John preached, "Someone greater than me is coming. I am not worthy to remove His sandals. **I baptize you with water, but He will**

baptize you with the Holy Spirit."

By this time, Jesus was an adult. He went to see John the Baptist at the Jordan River. When John saw Jesus, he said, "Here is the Lamb of God, who takes away the sin of the world!"

Jesus told John that He wanted to be baptized. But John didn't think he should baptize Jesus. "I need You to baptize me," John said. "Why do You want me to baptize You?" John was confused. **He baptized people who confessed their sins; Jesus never sinned!**

Jesus said, "Allow Me to be baptized. God says this is right." So John agreed, and he baptized Jesus.

Jesus immediately came up out of the water. Suddenly, the heavens opened and Jesus saw the Holy Spirit coming down on Him like a dove. God's voice came from heaven. "This is My Son," the voice said. "I love Him, and I am very pleased with Him!"

Christ Connection: Jesus never sinned, but He obeyed God and was baptized like sinners are baptized. Baptism reminds us of Jesus' death and resurrection. It reminds us that when we trust in Jesus, we turn from sin and start a new life—a life lived for Jesus.

Bible Storytelling Tips

- **Use gestures:** Hold up your arms when speaking John's dialogue.
- **Display art:** Show the Bible story picture and point to elements of the scene at appropriate points in the story.

INTRODUCE the Story

SESSION TITLE: Jesus' Baptism
BIBLE PASSAGE: Matthew 3; Mark 1; Luke 3; John 1
STORY POINT: Jesus obeyed God by being baptized.
KEY PASSAGE: John 3:30
BIG PICTURE QUESTION: Why did Jesus become human? Jesus became human to obey His Father's plan and rescue sinners.

Welcome time

Note: Be sensitive to kids who may have difficult family backgrounds.

Greet each kid as he or she arrives. Use this time to collect the offering, fill out attendance sheets, and help new kids connect to your group. Prompt kids to discuss things that make their parents happy.

SAY • One thing that parents really appreciate is obedience. Kids can do many things to make their parents happy, but obeying them is definitely near the top of the list. Today we will learn about something Jesus did to obey God. How do you think God responded to Jesus?

Activity page (5 minutes)

· "Descending Like A..." activity page, 1 per kid
· pencils or markers

Invite kids to complete the "Descending Like A ..." activity page. Kids will draw lines connecting the dots in numerical order to reveal a picture of a dove.

SAY • In our story today, we will hear about a time the Spirit of God came down onto Jesus. The Bible says He came down like a dove. When do you think this happened, and why? We'll learn more soon.

Session starter (10 minutes)

LOW PREP

OPTION 1: Paper dove-planes

· paper

Provide each kid with a sheet of paper. Challenge the kids to make paper airplanes that will stand in for doves. The goal for each kid is to make an airplane that takes longest to "float" to the ground.

SAY • Great job on those paper doves. They really looked graceful floating to the ground! Today we will hear about a time the Holy Spirit came down from heaven like a dove onto Jesus, and God the Father spoke! We'll hear the whole story soon.

OPTION 2: Pom-pom bugs

· pom-poms
· chenille stems
· googly eyes
· glue sticks
· scissors (optional)

Provide pom-poms, chenille stems, googly eyes, and glue sticks. Encourage the kids to make their own unique bugs using the pom-poms as the abdomens and chenille stems as legs. You may provide scissors for kids to cut the legs into shorter lengths.

SAY • Those are some cute bugs! Today we will learn about John the Baptist. He lived in the wilderness and ate locusts, which are basically very large grasshoppers. Our bugs wouldn't be very tasty, but then again, a locust probably wouldn't be either! We'll learn why John was called "the Baptist" and about a special man he baptized.

Transition to teach the story

TEACH the Story

SESSION TITLE: Jesus' Baptism
BIBLE PASSAGE: Matthew 3; Mark 1; Luke 3; John 1
STORY POINT: Jesus obeyed God by being baptized.
KEY PASSAGE: John 3:30
BIG PICTURE QUESTION: Why did Jesus become human? Jesus became human to obey His Father's plan and rescue sinners.

· room decorations
· Theme Background Slide (optional)

Suggested Theme Decorating Ideas: Decorate the stage to look like a road construction site. Set up traffic cones around the stage and use caution tape to separate certain areas of the stage from other areas. You may display the theme background slide.

Countdown

· countdown video

Show the countdown video as you transition to teach the story. Set it to end as the session begins.

Introduce the session (3 minutes)

· leader attire
· reflective vest
· hard hat

Tip: If you prefer not to use themed content or characters, adapt or omit this introduction.

[Leader enters wearing blue jeans, a T-shirt with a reflective vest, and a hard hat.]

LEADER • Careful, friends! I haven't seen y'all around here before, and construction sites can be dangerous. As long as you don't cross the caution tape, you should be fine without hard hats. We've been digging up the old roads so we can lay the foundations of the new roads.

Yeah, it really used to be pothole central around here. Thankfully, the city finally ponied up the funds to fix the streets. My job last week was running the jackhammer to break up the old, run-down pavement. My buddy would then gather the chunks into a wheelbarrow and carry them to a pile where the dump trucks would collect the debris to carry away.

It's a lot of work to fix up a road, but it's worth it to have a smooth, easy trip around the city. We prepare the way so people can come into our great city without too much trouble. In a way, that reminds me of a Bible story. Before Jesus started His ministry on earth, a man named John prepared the way. Let me tell you more about it!

Big picture question (1 minute)

LEADER • For the next few weeks, we'll be looking at a big picture question that will help us better understand the stories we learn. *Why did Jesus become human? Jesus became human to obey His Father's plan and rescue sinners*. We'll see in this story that everything Jesus did was to obey and glorify God. Jesus stepped down from His rightful place in heaven in order to live as a human and make the way for humans to live forever with God.

Giant timeline (1 minute)

Show the giant timeline. Point to individual Bible stories as you review.

· Giant Timeline

LEADER • In the beginning, God created a perfect world and had a perfect relationship with Adam and Eve, the people He created to live in His world. When they chose to sin, it broke their relationship with God and messed up everything in creation. God still loved them though, and He had a plan to fix everything. God raised up a nation—the Israelites—and promised to send a Rescuer through them.

After thousands of years, the time had come, and Jesus was born into the world. He was fully human and fully God, and He grew into a man. When the time was right, He began His public teaching and ministry by being baptized. I'll tell you about it.

Tell the Bible story (10 minutes)

- Bibles
- "Jesus' Baptism" video
- Big Picture Question Poster
- Bible Story Picture Poster
- Story Point Poster

Open your Bible to Matthew 3; Mark 1; Luke 3; John 1. Use the Bible storytelling tips on the Bible story page to help you tell the story, or show the Bible story video "Jesus' Baptism."

LEADER • In those days, baptism was used as a symbol to show that you needed to be cleansed of your old sinful choices so that you could obey God better. John told people to repent, or turn away from, their sin and be baptized.

John's job was to prepare the way for Jesus. John reminded people that the Messiah would come soon. John's preaching was getting people ready to meet Jesus and hear from Him. He knew that Jesus was the most important, and John wanted people to know that too.

When Jesus showed up, John knew who He was. Jesus' request to be baptized shocked John. Jesus had no sin to repent of. But Jesus knew baptism was part of God's plan. **Jesus obeyed God by being baptized**, and Jesus' baptism led to God's announcement of Jesus' identity as His Son. The Holy Spirit rested on Jesus, and God's rescue plan entered a new phase.

Christ connection

LEADER • Jesus never sinned, but He obeyed God and was baptized like sinners are baptized. Baptism reminds us of Jesus' death and resurrection. It reminds us that when we trust in Jesus, we turn from sin and start a new life—a life lived for Jesus. Baptism also shows the world that we are part of Jesus' family.

When a person has decided to love and worship Jesus as her Savior and King, she will choose to be baptized to show the world outwardly the change God has done inside her heart. Going into the water and coming back out shows a picture of Jesus' burial and resurrection. The Bible teaches us that believing in Jesus means we "die" to our old lives and are raised to life as new creations.

Note: You may use this opportunity to use Scripture and the guide provided to explain how to become a Christian. Make sure kids know when and where they can ask questions.

Questions from kids video (3 minutes)

Show the "Unit 20, Session 1" questions from kids video. Prompt kids to think about why baptism is important. Guide them to discuss questions they may still have about baptism.

· "Unit 20, Session 1" Questions from Kids video

Missions moment (3 minutes)

Play the "Introduction to MAF" missions video.

LEADER • Some villages are very hard to reach by car and would take days to hike to on foot. That's where the Mission Aviation Fellowship comes in. Pilots who love Jesus and want to tell the world about Him can fly small airplanes into these faraway villages. We know that **Jesus obeyed God by being baptized**. Many people have heard about Jesus and chosen to be baptized because of MAF.

· "Introduction to MAF" missions video

Say a prayer for the MAF pilots and any missionaries your church supports.

Key passage (5 minutes)

· Key Passage Poster
· "He Must Increase,
but I Must Decrease
(John 3:30)" song

Show the key passage poster. Lead the boys and girls to read together John 3:30. Sing "He Must Increase, but I Must Decrease (John 3:30)."

LEADER • This key passage comes from the Gospel of John, but it was spoken by John the Baptist, a different John than the man who wrote that book of the Bible. John the Baptist was reminding people who had followed him that he was not the most important. John's job was to prepare people for Jesus. With Jesus around, John wanted to become less important and let Jesus get the glory and attention He deserves.

Sing (4 minutes)

· "Jesus Messiah" song

LEADER • Jesus is the Messiah. He perfectly obeyed God and died a death He did not deserve so we could be rescued from sin. He deserves all our praise.

Sing together "Jesus Messiah."

Pray (2 minutes)

Invite kids to pray before dismissing to apply the story.

LEADER • Thank You, God, for sending Jesus to save us. Thank You that He perfectly obeyed You in all things, from baptism even to death on the cross. Help us obey You through our love for You. Amen.

Dismiss to apply the story

The Gospel: God's Plan for Me

Ask kids if they have ever heard the word *gospel*. Clarify that the word *gospel* means "good news." It is the message about Christ, the kingdom of God, and salvation. Use the following guide to share the gospel with kids.

God rules. Explain to kids that the Bible tells us God created everything, and He is in charge of everything. Invite a volunteer to read Genesis 1:1 from the Bible. Read Revelation 4:11 or Colossians 1:16-17 aloud and explain what these verses mean.

We sinned. Tell kids that since the time of Adam and Eve, everyone has chosen to disobey God. (Romans 3:23) The Bible calls this sin. Because God is holy, God cannot be around sin. Sin separates us from God and deserves God's punishment of death. (Romans 6:23)

God provided. Choose a child to read John 3:16 aloud. Say that God sent His Son, Jesus, the perfect solution to our sin problem, to rescue us from the punishment we deserve. It's something we, as sinners, could never earn on our own. Jesus alone saves us. Read and explain Ephesians 2:8-9.

Jesus gives. Share with kids that Jesus lived a perfect life, died on the cross for our sins, and rose again. Because Jesus gave up His life for us, we can be welcomed into God's family for eternity. This is the best gift ever! Read Romans 5:8; 2 Corinthians 5:21; or 1 Peter 3:18.

We respond. Tell kids that they can respond to Jesus. Read Romans 10:9-10,13. Review these aspects of our response: Believe in your heart that Jesus alone saves you through what He's already done on the cross. Repent, turning from self and sin to Jesus. Tell God and others that your faith is in Jesus.

Offer to talk with any child who is interested in responding to Jesus. Provide *I'm a Christian Now!* for new Christians to take home and complete with their families.

APPLY the Story

SESSION TITLE: Jesus' Baptism

BIBLE PASSAGE: Matthew 3; Mark 1; Luke 3; John 1

STORY POINT: Jesus obeyed God by being baptized.

KEY PASSAGE: John 3:30

BIG PICTURE QUESTION: Why did Jesus become human? Jesus became human to obey His Father's plan and rescue sinners.

Key passage activity (5 minutes)

· Key Passage Poster

Tip: Consider using sign language to increase inclusivity.

Work with the kids to develop hand motions that go with the key passage. Say the key passage multiple times using the hand motions to help kids remember the passage. You may use the suggested motions below.

Suggested motions:
- He [*Point up towards heaven.*]
- must increase [*Move hands apart.*]
- I [*Point to yourself with both thumbs.*]
- must decrease [*Move hands together.*]

SAY • This key passage is short, but very important. John the Baptist spoke these words about Jesus when many people who were following John began to follow Jesus instead. John knew that his job was to point people to Jesus, not to take glory for himself. That's our job too!

Discussion & Bible skills (10 minutes)

· Bibles, 1 per kid
· Story Point Poster
· Small Group Timeline and Map Set
(005802970, optional)

Distribute a Bible to each kid. Help them find Matthew 3. Remind the kids that Matthew is the first book in the New Testament in the Gospels division. You may use the New Testament Israel Map to show where Galilee is. (C5)

Ask the following questions. Lead the group to discuss:

Option: Retell or review the Bible story using the bolded text of the Bible story script.

1. Who was John the Baptist? (*the one Isaiah prophesied about, the voice crying out in the wilderness; Matt. 3:3*)

2. How did John respond at first to Jesus' request for baptism? (*John tried to stop Jesus at first, Matt. 3:14*)

3. What happened after Jesus was baptized? (*God spoke from heaven, and the Holy Spirit descended like a dove; Matt. 3:16-17*)

4. Does baptism save us? *Guide the kids to understand that baptism is important, but it is only a symbol of what Jesus has done for us. A person is baptized because she is saved, not in order to be saved. Suggest an analogy, such as dressing like a doctor versus being a doctor. Dressing the part can suggest you are a doctor but cannot make you a doctor if you are not one.*

5. Why is baptism important? *Help kids understand that God has commanded believers to be baptized, and Jesus provided an example of baptism for us to follow. We do not obey God to earn our salvation, but we want to obey Him out of love and worship. Baptism is a beautiful picture of our sinful lives dying with Jesus and our new life beginning when we are "raised" from the water. It shows the world we trust Jesus and identify with Him.*

6. When should someone be baptized? *Discuss with your kids whatever policies your church has in place regarding baptism. Remind kids that baptism is a way to show they have trusted Christ; anyone who has not trusted Christ should not be baptized. Direct kids to continue the discussion with their parents to decide if or when they should be baptized.*

SAY • **Jesus obeyed God by being baptized.** When we trust Jesus for salvation, we obey God this way too.

Activity choice (10 minutes)

OPTION 1: The Mission Aviation Fellowship (MAF) Give each kid a copy of the "Welcome to MAF" printable and crayons or pencils. Ask a volunteer to read the story at the top of the page aloud. Help kids unscramble the words. (*airplanes, world, love, people, villages*) Then ask another volunteer to read the decoded message aloud.

SAY • The missionary pilots and the other MAF workers are able to share Jesus' love with people whom no one can reach! They can deliver food and medical supplies, transport people to hospitals, and most importantly, they can teach people about Jesus.

Ask parents or church members to donate travel-size toiletry items for a mission project included in Session 3 of Unit 20.

OPTION 2: Prepare the way

Hold a length of cardboard at a slight incline to serve as a track for the toy cars. Place small obstacles like paper wads, cotton balls, and so forth on the track. Let kids predict how long the car will take to reach the bottom. Then allow a kid to remove the obstacles before sending the car down the track again.

SAY • The toy car was able to make it to the bottom much more easily when the obstacles were removed. When we "prepared the way," it rolled down better. In a similar way, John's job was to prepare people for Jesus by telling people the Messiah was coming and by preaching about repentance and God's kingdom. When **Jesus obeyed God by being baptized**, God proclaimed that Jesus was His Son, and the Holy Spirit rested on Jesus like a dove. The people could remember what John had said and see that Jesus was

---

LOW PREP

· "Welcome to MAF" printable
· crayons or pencils

Tip: Use this activity option to reinforce the missions moment found in Teach the Story.

· small toy cars
· long cardboard track
· small obstacles (paper wads, cotton balls, and so forth)

the Messiah that God had promised long ago. When we show people love and teach them about the gospel, we are preparing the way for the Holy Spirit to change their hearts to love and worship Jesus.

Reflection and prayer (5 minutes)

Distribute a sheet of paper to each child. Ask the kids to write about or draw a picture to answer the following questions:

- What does this story teach me about God or about the gospel?
- What does this story teach me about myself?
- Whom can I tell about this story?

Make sure to send the sheets home with kids alongside the activity page so that parents can see what their kids have been learning.

If time remains, take prayer requests or allow kids to complete the Bible story coloring page provided with this session. Pray for your group.

· pencils and crayons
· paper
· Bible Story Coloring Page, 1 per kid

Tip: Give parents this week's *Big Picture Cards for Families* to allow families to interact with the biblical content at home.

Easter · Session 2
Jesus' Crucifixion and Resurrection

BIBLE PASSAGE:
Matthew 26–28; 1 Corinthians 15

STORY POINT:
Jesus' resurrection gives us hope for eternal life.

KEY PASSAGE:
John 3:30

BIG PICTURE QUESTION:
Why did Jesus become human? Jesus became human to obey His Father's plan and rescue sinners.

INTRODUCE THE STORY (10–15 MINUTES) PAGE 102	**TEACH THE STORY** (25–30 MINUTES) PAGE 104	**APPLY THE STORY** (25–30 MINUTES) PAGE 110

 → →

Additional resources are available at gospelproject.com. For free training and session-by-session help, visit MinistryGrid.com/thegospelproject.

LEADER Bible Study

Jesus' crucifixion and resurrection are essential to the Christian faith. If we teach Jesus as a respected teacher and miracle-worker who claimed to be the Messiah and who was crucified on the cross—but who was not resurrected—then we are teaching the Jesus of Judaism. If we teach Jesus as a wise teacher and prophet who ascended into heaven—but who was not crucified—then we are teaching the Jesus of Islam.

Jesus' purpose for coming to earth was to save us from our sins. (Matt. 1:21) Jesus came to die to show God's love to us (Rom. 5:7-8) so that whoever believes in Him will not perish but have eternal life. (John 3:16) Jesus came to die so that we would be forgiven. (Eph. 1:7) Jesus came to die to bring us to God. (1 Pet. 3:18)

Jesus died on the cross to satisfy the wrath of God toward sin. His resurrection proved that God was satisfied with Jesus' sacrifice. If Jesus had died but not been raised up, He would have been like military leaders who died without a throne. (Acts 5:33-37) But Jesus conquered death, just as He said He would. (John 2:19-21) If there was no resurrection, Paul says, our faith would be worthless. We would be dead in our sins. (1 Cor. 15:17)

But Jesus' resurrection gives us hope for our resurrection. The same Spirit that raised Jesus from the dead will raise our bodies to life. (Rom. 8:11)

Jesus' crucifixion and resurrection are not the end of the story, but the center of it. As you teach kids this Bible story, emphasize the gospel: the good news of who Jesus is and what He has done. We do not worship a dead Savior. Jesus is alive! There is hope for sinners. Jesus' resurrection gives believers the promise of new life. "For as in Adam all die, so also in Christ all will be made alive" (1 Cor. 15:22).

Easter

The **BIBLE** Story

Jesus' Crucifixion and Resurrection
Matthew 26–28; 1 Corinthians 15

After Jesus was arrested, He was led to the high priest. The religious leaders were trying to find a reason to kill Jesus, but they could not. **The high priest asked, "Are You the Messiah, the Son of God?" Jesus replied, "Yes, that's right."**

The high priest said, "He has spoken against God! He deserves to die!" The religious leaders refused to believe that Jesus was God's Son.

In the morning, the religious leaders led Jesus to Pilate, the governor. "Are You the King of the Jews?" Pilate asked.

"Yes, that's right," Jesus replied.

"What should I do with Jesus?" Pilate asked the crowd. "Crucify Him!" they answered. Pilate did not think Jesus had done anything wrong, but he handed Jesus over and said, "Do whatever you want."

The governor's soldiers put a scarlet robe on Jesus. They made a crown of thorns and put it on His head. Then they mocked Him: "Here is the King of the Jews!" They beat Jesus and led Him away to be killed.

The soldiers nailed Jesus to a cross. They put a sign above His head that said THIS IS JESUS, THE KING OF THE JEWS. **Two**

criminals were crucified next to Him.

Darkness covered the land. **Jesus cried out, "My God, My God, why have You forsaken Me?" Jesus shouted again and then He died.** Suddenly, the curtain in the temple sanctuary split in two, from top to bottom, and there was an earthquake. One of the men guarding Jesus' body said, "This man really was God's Son!"

Jesus was buried in a tomb. A stone was sealed in front of the tomb so that no one could steal Jesus' body.

On the third day, Mary Magdalene (MAG duh leen) **and the other Mary went to the tomb.** Suddenly there was an earthquake. **An angel of the Lord rolled back the stone and sat on it.** The guards were so afraid that they fainted.

The angel spoke to the women, "Don't be afraid! I know you are looking for Jesus. He is not here. He has risen, just like He said He would."

The women left the tomb quickly. They **ran to tell the disciples the good news. Just then Jesus greeted them.** The women worshiped Him. "Don't be afraid," Jesus told them. "Tell My followers to go to Galilee. They will see Me there."

Jesus appeared to Peter and then to the other disciples. Jesus also appeared to more than 500 people who followed Him. **Many people witnessed that Jesus is alive!**

Christ Connection: Jesus' death and resurrection is the center of the gospel. In Adam, we were spiritually dead in sin, but Jesus died to pay for our sins. Jesus is alive! God gives new life to everyone who trusts in Jesus.

Bible Storytelling Tips

• **Draw pictures:** Sketch symbols as you tell the story—a question mark for Jesus' trial, a cross for His death, a rising sun for His resurrection, and so on.

• **Use lighting effects:** Begin the story with lights dimmed. Raise the lights when telling of Jesus' resurrection.

INTRODUCE the Story

SESSION TITLE: Jesus' Crucifixion and Resurrection

BIBLE PASSAGE: Matthew 26–28; 1 Corinthians 15

STORY POINT: Jesus' resurrection gives us hope for eternal life.

KEY PASSAGE: John 3:30

BIG PICTURE QUESTION: Why did Jesus become human? Jesus became human to obey His Father's plan and rescue sinners.

Welcome time

Greet each kid as he or she arrives. Use this time to collect the offering, fill out attendance sheets, and help new kids connect to your group. Prompt kids to discuss what their family does to celebrate Easter. Steer conversations away from secular traditions to help kids focus on the true reason for Easter.

SAY • Easter is a wonderful holiday on which we celebrate the most amazing thing that has ever happened: Jesus' resurrection from the dead. Many people have different ways they celebrate Easter, but Christians all over the world are all celebrating the same thing: Jesus' victory over death!

Activity page (5 minutes)

· "Bleak and Beautiful" activity page, 1 per kid

· pencils or markers

Invite kids to complete the "Bleak and Beautiful" activity page. Guide kids to color the sheet according to the number key.

SAY • The day Jesus died on the cross is called Good Friday. It was a very sad day, but we call it good because it was the day Jesus took our place and died on the cross for our sins. It was both sad and beautiful.

Session starter (10 minutes)

OPTION 1: Crime and punishment

Direct the kids to come up with silly rules and silly punishments to go along with those rules if they are broken. For example, you could say that there is a new rule that you may not bend your elbows; if you bend your elbows, you will have to hold your hands over your head for two days.

SAY • Those crimes were silly, and the silly punishments fit alongside the crimes. Today we will learn about Jesus. His punishment was severe and very serious, but He did not commit any crime at all. Why do you think Jesus was punished severely if He was not guilty?

OPTION 2: Empty tomb

Use chairs and tables to provide structure for a pillow fort. Stack pillows or cushions against the furniture and drape blankets over the structure to make a kind of "cave." Allow the kids to take turns going into the cave. To ensure everyone's safety, do not allow any kids to play unsupervised in the pillow fort and ensure no adult leader enters the fort one-on-one with a kid.

· chairs and tables
· pillows or cushions
· blankets

SAY • Jesus died on the cross and was buried in a tomb. Jesus' tomb would have been kind of like a cave; the Bible tells us it was cut into the side of a rocky hill. We took turns going into out little tomb and coming out, and today we will hear about how Jesus came out of His tomb. A little while later, some other people also went in the tomb and came out.

Transition to teach the story

TEACH the Story

SESSION TITLE: Jesus' Crucifixion and Resurrection

BIBLE PASSAGE: Matthew 26–28; 1 Corinthians 15

STORY POINT: Jesus' resurrection gives us hope for eternal life.

KEY PASSAGE: John 3:30

BIG PICTURE QUESTION: Why did Jesus become human? Jesus became human to obey His Father's plan and rescue sinners.

Countdown

· countdown video

Show the countdown video as you transition to teach the story. Set it to end as the session begins.

Introduce the session (3 minutes)

· leader attire
· reflective vest
· hard hat

[Leader enters wearing blue jeans, a T-shirt with a reflective vest, and a hard hat.]

Tip: If you prefer not to use themed content or characters, adapt or omit this introduction.

LEADER • Hey there, friends. I've got some great news for you. It's Easter! I'm all dressed for work, but I actually have today off. I just think these reflective vests are cool. I'm not the only one either, as I saw a lot of folks in the parking lot wearing them too.

When I was a kid, I never really got as excited about Easter as I did for some other holidays like Christmas. But the reason was I didn't fully understand how amazing the good news of Jesus really is. Eventually, when I did understand what Easter is all about, I saw that it's just as exciting as Christmas, and more exciting than just about any other holiday!

You see, Easter isn't just a time to use bright colors and enjoy springtime weather. Christmas is a celebration of the fact that Jesus came to earth as a human, and Easter is a time to remember and celebrate why He came. Here, I'll tell you all about it!

Big picture question (1 minute)

LEADER • As we get into the story, we should say our big picture question and answer. Can you all say it with me? [*Allow responses.*] Great! ***Why did Jesus become human? Jesus became human to obey His Father's plan and rescue sinners***. God had a plan since before the creation of the world. His plan included sending Jesus, His own Son, to earth as a human. Jesus obeyed and came as a human so that He could perfectly understand our suffering and pain that comes from sin and live the sinless life we fail to live. He then died on the cross for our sins and rose again to defeat death. That's how He rescued sinners!

Giant timeline (1 minute)

Show the giant timeline. Point to individual Bible stories as you review.

· Giant Timeline

LEADER • Last week we talked about Jesus' baptism. That was the start of Jesus' public ministry. Before that, He was basically living a normal but perfectly sinless life. **Jesus obeyed God by being baptized**, and God spoke from heaven to say that Jesus is His Son and God is pleased with Him. Then the Holy Spirit rested on Jesus like a dove. Today, we are going to jump ahead a bit to talk about what exactly God had planned.

Tell the Bible story (10 minutes)

· "Jesus' Crucifixion and Resurrection" video
· Big Picture Question Poster
· Bible Story Picture Poster
· Story Point Poster

Open your Bible to Matthew 26–28; 1 Corinthians 15. Use the Bible storytelling tips on the Bible story page to help you tell the story, or show the Bible story video "Jesus' Crucifixion and Resurrection."

LEADER • He is risen! For thousands of years, Christians have used this phrase as a greeting and a way to declare the good news. When you hear a person say "He is risen," you can respond by saying "He is risen indeed." Let's try that together; I'll say the first part, and you respond with the second part. Ready? He is Risen! [*Allow responses, coaxing kids to say "He is risen indeed."*] Great job!

The crucifixion of Jesus and His resurrection on the third day make up the center of the one big story of the Bible. Ever since Adam and Eve chose to rebel against God and eat the fruit He commanded them not to eat, all of creation has been broken. People could no longer have a loving relationship with God without multiple sacrifices every year. For generations, it seemed as though evil might eventually win. When Jesus—the only perfect Person, who is God the Son—died, it looked like evil actually had won. But in a wonderful turn of events, God brought about the ultimate defeat of sin and death when Jesus' heart began to beat and His lungs filled with fresh breath. Jesus was alive!

He is still alive today. He will never again die because His sacrifice for sin is perfect and complete. He took the punishment of God's anger for sin on Himself. He died with it, taking it away from everyone who believes in Him. Then He rose from the dead without it. The sin stayed dead, but Jesus did not. Now we can live forever too. **Jesus' resurrection gives us hope for eternal life.**

Christ connection

LEADER • Jesus' death and resurrection is the center of the gospel. In Adam, we were spiritually dead in sin, but Jesus died to pay for our sins. Jesus is alive! God gives new life to everyone who trusts in Jesus. The Bible tells us that when we trust in Jesus, our sin was put to death with Jesus, and we have new, resurrected hearts.

Note: You may use this opportunity to use Scripture and the guide provided to explain how to become a Christian. Make sure kids know when and where they can ask questions.

Questions from kids video (3 minutes)

Show the "Easter, Session 2" questions from kids video. Prompt kids to think about why we forgive others. Guide them to discuss if there are ever times we do not have to forgive others.

· "Easter, Session 2" Questions from Kids video

Missions moment (3 minutes)

Show "The Gospel" missions video. Ask kids to describe things we can tell other people about Jesus. (*He was born on earth; He is fully God and fully human; He died on a cross for our sins; He rose to life; He wants everyone to be with Him in heaven forever; and so forth.*)

· "The Gospel" missions video

LEADER • The gospel—the good news of Jesus—is the reason that missionaries go all over the world. They want to be obedient to take the gospel to all people, even those who are very hard to reach. Missionaries sacrifice a lot so other people can know that **Jesus' resurrection gives us hope for eternal life.**

Key passage (5 minutes)

· Key Passage Poster
· "He Must Increase, but I Must Decrease (John 3:30)" song

Show the key passage poster. Lead the boys and girls to read together John 3:30. Then sing "He Must Increase, but I Must Decrease (John 3:30)."

LEADER • John the Baptist knew that Jesus is most important. John did not want his life to be about bringing glory to himself. He wanted to give all glory to Jesus, the only Person who deserves all glory! That's why John said that he must decrease while Jesus must increase.

Sing (4 minutes)

· "Take It to the Lord" song

LEADER • In the Bible, Jesus teaches that there is no greater way to show love than to sacrifice your life to save someone else's. Jesus showed this love perfectly when He died for our sins and rose again to give us eternal life. Let's praise Him, the best friend we can have.

Sing together "Take It to the Lord."

Pray (2 minutes)

Invite kids to pray before dismissing to apply the story.

LEADER • Father, thank You for the wonderful gift of salvation. We know that we could never earn such a perfect love. We praise You for giving it to us anyway. Help us love You and celebrate what Jesus has done. Give us hearts that want to obey. Amen.

Dismiss to apply the story

The Gospel: God's Plan for Me

Ask kids if they have ever heard the word *gospel*. Clarify that the word *gospel* means "good news." It is the message about Christ, the kingdom of God, and salvation. Use the following guide to share the gospel with kids.

God rules. Explain to kids that the Bible tells us God created everything, and He is in charge of everything. Invite a volunteer to read Genesis 1:1 from the Bible. Read Revelation 4:11 or Colossians 1:16-17 aloud and explain what these verses mean.

We sinned. Tell kids that since the time of Adam and Eve, everyone has chosen to disobey God. (Romans 3:23) The Bible calls this sin. Because God is holy, God cannot be around sin. Sin separates us from God and deserves God's punishment of death. (Romans 6:23)

God provided. Choose a child to read John 3:16 aloud. Say that God sent His Son, Jesus, the perfect solution to our sin problem, to rescue us from the punishment we deserve. It's something we, as sinners, could never earn on our own. Jesus alone saves us. Read and explain Ephesians 2:8-9.

Jesus gives. Share with kids that Jesus lived a perfect life, died on the cross for our sins, and rose again. Because Jesus gave up His life for us, we can be welcomed into God's family for eternity. This is the best gift ever! Read Romans 5:8; 2 Corinthians 5:21; or 1 Peter 3:18.

We respond. Tell kids that they can respond to Jesus. Read Romans 10:9-10,13. Review these aspects of our response: Believe in your heart that Jesus alone saves you through what He's already done on the cross. Repent, turning from self and sin to Jesus. Tell God and others that your faith is in Jesus.

Offer to talk with any child who is interested in responding to Jesus. Provide *I'm a Christian Now!* for new Christians to take home and complete with their families.

APPLY the Story

SESSION TITLE: Jesus' Crucifixion and Resurrection

BIBLE PASSAGE: Matthew 26–28; 1 Corinthians 15

STORY POINT: Jesus' resurrection gives us hope for eternal life.

KEY PASSAGE: John 3:30

BIG PICTURE QUESTION: Why did Jesus become human? Jesus became human to obey His Father's plan and rescue sinners.

Key passage activity (5 minutes)

· Key Passage Poster
· stopwatch

Say the key passage as a group multiple times. Use the motions developed in the first session. Use a stopwatch to see how quickly the kids can say the verse without fumbling the motions. Thank all the kids for their efforts and encourage the kids to keep working to memorize the passage. You may also challenge the kids to say the verse in "slow motion," to see if they can stretch the short verse over 10 seconds, 20 seconds, or more.

SAY • John knew that his purpose was to point others to Jesus so that Jesus would be glorified. We have the same role. We can glorify Jesus in our lives and point others to Him.

Discussion & Bible skills (10 minutes)

· Bibles, 1 per kid
· Story Point Poster
· Small Group Timeline and Map Set (005802970, optional)

Distribute a Bible to each kid. Help the kids use the table of contents to find Matthew 26–28. Ask a volunteer to explain what division Matthew is in, and what that division contains. (*the Gospels; the stories of Jesus' life, ministry, death, and resurrection*) You may select a strong reader to read a few verses of your choosing from those chapters, such as Matthew 27:50-51; 28:5-6.

Ask the following questions. Lead the group to discuss:

Option: Retell or review the Bible story using the bolded text of the Bible story script.

1. What did the religious leaders want to do with Jesus? (*kill Him, Matt. 26:66*)

2. What sign was hung above Jesus on the cross? (*THIS IS JESUS, KING OF THE JEWS, Matt 27:37*)

3. Who saw Jesus raised from the dead? (*Mary Magdalene, Peter and the disciples, and more than 500 other people; Matt. 28:1,16; 1 Cor. 15:5-8*)

4. How can you know if you are saved? *Guide kids to see it is not our feelings that save us, it is God's grace given to us through faith. (Eph. 2:8-9) Help them understand that salvation comes to everyone who trusts in Jesus. (Rom. 10:9) Explain what is written in the Bible—we can know that we are saved, even if we don't feel saved or do sometimes choose sin. (1 John 5:12-13)*

5. Why is the resurrection so important? *Discuss Jesus' role as a substitute. Jesus died for our sins because He had no sin. If He had stayed dead, it would have meant His sacrifice wasn't enough. Jesus' resurrection ensures that we will live forever with God because it proved that sin is paid for completely.*

6. What does it mean to have eternal life? *Help kids understand that eternal life is more than just a place with God after we die. Point out that our new life begins as soon as we believe the truth about Jesus. We become new creatures. Our current lives reflect that change through loving obedience to Jesus, and we look to the future when Jesus will return and fix all that sin has broken.*

SAY • **Jesus' resurrection gives us hope for eternal life**. Eternal life isn't just for some point in the future but begins right away as our lives change to glorify God.

Activity choice (10 minutes)

- small flower pots
- markers
- stickers or other craft supplies for decorating

OPTION 1: Giving seeds

Distribute small flower pots and invite each kid to decorate a flower pot to use at home to collect coins to donate. Remind your kids about any special Easter collections your church participates in, or plan a special collection for the next few weeks to donate to missionaries your church supports.

Tip: Use this activity option to reinforce the missions moment found in Teach the Story.

SAY • Giving money is one way that we can support missionaries. That's why our church gives offerings to missions. We can help provide things like food, transportation, housing, and Bibles in different languages. It's one way that we can help missionaries who share the message that **Jesus' resurrection gives us hope for eternal life**. Even a small amount given can help provide the seeds needed to grow a thriving ministry.

Ask parents or church members to donate travel-size toiletry items for a mission project included in session 3 of unit 20.

LOW PREP

OPTION 2: Resurrection tag

Select a kid to be *It*. He will chase the other kids to tag them. When a kid is tagged, she must sit on the ground. Untagged kids may bring tagged kids back into the game by tapping the tagged kid gently on the shoulder and saying **Jesus' resurrection gives us hope for eternal life**. Play as time allows, rotating which kid is *It* every few minutes.

SAY • In our game, being tagged meant you were out of the game—at least for a while. But hearing the good news about Jesus let you get back into the game. In a way this is similar to our lives. We are born in sin. Through Adam, all of us have sinful hearts that choose to disobey God. But the good news is that Jesus died on the cross and rose again. Through Jesus, we can all have new life today and forever into the future. **Jesus' resurrection gives us hope for eternal life.**

Reflection and prayer (5 minutes)

Distribute a sheet of paper to each child. Ask the kids to write about or draw a picture to answer the following questions:

- What does this story teach me about God or about the gospel?
- What does this story teach me about myself?
- Whom can I tell about this story?

Make sure to send the sheets home with kids alongside the activity page so that parents can see what their kids have been learning.

If time remains, take prayer requests or allow kids to complete the Bible story coloring page provided with this session. Pray for your group.

· pencils and crayons
· paper
· Bible Story Coloring Page, 1 per kid

Tip: Give parents this week's *Big Picture Cards for Families* to allow families to interact with the biblical content at home.

Use Week of:

Unit 20 · Session 2
Jesus' Temptation

BIBLE PASSAGE:
Matthew 4; Mark 1; Luke 4

STORY POINT:
Jesus was tempted and never sinned.

KEY PASSAGE:
John 3:30

BIG PICTURE QUESTION:
Why did Jesus become human? Jesus became human to obey His Father's plan and rescue sinners.

INTRODUCE THE STORY
(10–15 MINUTES)
PAGE 118

→

TEACH THE STORY
(25–30 MINUTES)
PAGE 120

→

APPLY THE STORY
(25–30 MINUTES)
PAGE 126

Additional resources are available at gospelproject.com. For free training and session-by-session help, visit MinistryGrid.com/thegospelproject.

LEADER Bible Study

Satan wants to ruin God's plan. In Genesis 3, he tempted Adam and Eve to disobey God. Sin entered the world, and the perfect relationship between God and man was broken. But all along, God had a plan to rescue His people through His Son. So when Jesus came to earth, Satan didn't back down. After Jesus was baptized—beginning His ministry and effectively declaring war on Satan—Satan tempted Jesus.

If Satan could just get Jesus to stray from God's perfect plan—if he could just get Jesus to sin—then Jesus would be disqualified to be the sinless Savior people needed. But Satan could not stop God's plan.

Jesus' temptation is not primarily an example to be followed but more a declaration of who Jesus is. He is the answer to God's promise of a descendant who would crush the head of the snake. (Gen. 3:15) Jesus is the perfect sacrifice required to take away sin. Where Adam failed, Jesus succeeded. Adam brought guilt and death to the human race, but Jesus brings forgiveness and life to all who trust in Him.

Even today, the devil works hard "to steal and kill and destroy" (John 10:10). Teach kids that the power to resist temptation comes from Jesus. Kids may struggle to understand that following Jesus won't mean instant eradication of sin and temptation in our lives. (Sanctification is a lifelong process!) Pray that the kids you teach would see Jesus as their greatest treasure—more valuable than any instant gratification the world has to offer.

Finally, give kids hope for when they fail. Jesus' perfect obedience is credited to those who trust in Him. Remind the kids that "if we confess our sins, he [God] is faithful and righteous to forgive us our sins and to cleanse us from all unrighteousness" (1 John 1:9). We can boldly approach God's throne to receive both grace and mercy when we need it. (See Heb. 4:14-16.)

Jesus' Temptation

Matthew 4; Mark 1; Luke 4

After Jesus was baptized, the Holy Spirit led Him into the wilderness to be tempted by the devil. Jesus did not eat for 40 days and 40 nights. He prayed and thought about God's plan for His life. When those days were over, Jesus was hungry.

Then the devil, who tempts people to sin, came up to Jesus. He said, "If You are really God's Son, prove it. Tell these stones to become bread."

If Jesus used His power to turn the stones into bread, He could eat them so He wouldn't be hungry anymore. But Jesus refused. **Instead of using His own power, Jesus chose to trust God to meet His needs. Jesus said, "God's Word says that man must not live on bread alone but on every word that comes from the mouth of God."**

The devil tempted Jesus again. He took Jesus to the top of the temple in Jerusalem and said, "If You are really God's Son, prove it. Jump off this temple and trust God to protect You." **The devil even said: "God's Word says that God will order His angels to keep You safe, and they will protect You so that You will not even strike your foot against a stone."**

The devil had used words from Scripture, but Jesus knew the devil's command was foolish. **Jesus reminded him, "God's Word also says, do not test the Lord your God."**

Finally, the devil took Jesus to a high mountain. He showed Jesus all the kingdoms of the world and how great they were. The devil said to Jesus, "I will give You all the riches and power of these kingdoms. They belong to me, and I can give them to anyone I want. If You want them, **all You have to do is fall down and worship me."**

Jesus resisted temptation again. He replied, **"Go away, Satan! God's Word says: Worship the Lord your God and serve Him only."**

The devil left Jesus, and angels came right away to serve Jesus. Throughout all these temptations, **Jesus never sinned.**

Christ Connection: Jesus was tempted, but He trusted God and never sinned. Jesus is perfect and righteous. A perfect sacrifice was required to take away sin. Jesus was that perfect sacrifice. He died on the cross to free us from sin and to give us the power to say no to temptation.

Bible Storytelling Tips

- **Display a prop:** Each time you tell how Jesus responded to temptation, hold up the Bible.
- **Use dramatic conversation:** During dialogue, stand in various places for each speaker—Jesus and the devil.

INTRODUCE the Story

SESSION TITLE: Jesus' Temptation
BIBLE PASSAGE: Matthew 4; Mark 1; Luke 4
STORY POINT: Jesus was tempted and never sinned.
KEY PASSAGE: John 3:30
BIG PICTURE QUESTION: Why did Jesus become human? Jesus became human to obey His Father's plan and rescue sinners.

Welcome time

Greet each kid as he or she arrives. Use this time to collect the offering, fill out attendance sheets, and help new kids connect to your group. Prompt kids to talk about things they have never experienced or done before.

SAY • As you grow up, there are many new things you will do and see. Some of those things will be good, and some may be sad or difficult. One thing that everyone has done is sin against God. Everyone except Jesus, that is. Today we will learn about a time Jesus was tempted to sin. How do you think Jesus fought temptation?

Activity page (5 minutes)

· "Just Like Jesus" activity page, 1 per kid
· pencils or markers

Invite kids to complete the "Just Like Jesus" activity page. Guide kids to recreate the picture of Jesus, using the grid to help them draw the parts of the picture.

SAY • Great drawings. We are born in sin and are very unlike Jesus. But if we trust in Him and worship Him as our King, we can begin to fight temptation just as Jesus did! How else can we be just like Jesus?

Session starter (10 minutes)

OPTION 1: What is true?

Read the following sentences and instruct the kids to raise their hand if they think the sentence is true. If true, ask a kid or two to explain how they know. Consider making up your own sentences as well.

Suggested sentences:
- The United States of America was founded in 1776. (*true*)
- The Bible has 65 books. (*false, 66*)
- Plants create their own food using sunlight. (*true*)
- Saturn is the smallest planet in the solar system. (*false, Mercury*)

SAY • Sometimes it can be hard to know what is true. In our Bible story today, we will learn about a time Satan tried to trick Jesus so that Jesus would sin. Jesus knew the truth. How do you think Jesus defeated Satan's lies? We'll learn all about it soon.

OPTION 2: This or that?

Designate two sides of the room. You may hang signs that say *A* and *B*, *This* and *That*, or some other label. Ask kids about how they would act given different options, and instruct them to walk to the side of the room you assign to each option. Give kids a chance to explain their choices.

SAY • If we faced those situations in real life, we would probably be pretty tempted to choose the selfish, sinful option. Today we will learn about a time Jesus felt temptation. We will hear how Jesus fought back and chose to obey God.

· paper, pen, tape (optional)

Suggested options:
· keep a lost wallet or turn it into the lost and found
· copy a friend's homework or turn yours in unfinished
· befriend a new kid at school or stick with friends you know

Transition to teach the story

TEACH the Story

SESSION TITLE: Jesus' Temptation
BIBLE PASSAGE: Matthew 4; Mark 1; Luke 4
STORY POINT: Jesus was tempted and never sinned.
KEY PASSAGE: John 3:30
BIG PICTURE QUESTION: Why did Jesus become human? Jesus became human to obey His Father's plan and rescue sinners.

Countdown

· countdown video

Show the countdown video as you transition to teach the story. Set it to end as the session begins.

Introduce the session (3 minutes)

· leader attire
· reflective vest
· hard hat

Tip: If you prefer not to use themed content or characters, adapt or omit this introduction.

[Leader enters wearing bluejeans and a T-shirt with a reflective vest over it and a hard hat.]

LEADER • Hey, friends. I'm glad you made it here. My road work team and I have been working hard to get these roads fixed, but the hard thing is that, while the end goal is to fix some traffic issues, the work we do causes a lot of traffic issues in the meantime.

That's one of the big reasons it can be hard to start a project like road reconstruction. The temptation is to ignore the problems because, in the short term, stopping things to fix the problems makes the problems feel like bigger problems!

In a lot of situations, we face all sorts of temptations. In fact, even Jesus faced temptation to sin. The difference is, while we sometimes choose to disobey God, Jesus never did. Today, I want to share with you that story.

Big picture question (1 minute)

LEADER • Jesus faced temptation because Jesus is fully human. Our big picture question helps us understand the Father's plan. ***Why did Jesus become human? Jesus became human to obey His Father's plan and rescue sinners.*** Because the fair payment of sin is death, the only way for sinners to be saved is though the death of a perfect sacrifice. Because Jesus is fully human but never sinned, He was able to be the perfect sacrifice we needed.

Giant timeline (1 minute)

Show the giant timeline. Point to individual Bible stories as you review.

· Giant Timeline

LEADER • After Jesus was born as a human, He grew up. We learned a few weeks past that **Jesus obeyed God by being baptized**. Baptism is a picture of the death and resurrection of Jesus, and those who believe in Him are baptized to show the world they belong to Jesus. Last week, we specifically looked at the death and resurrection of Jesus. He was arrested and put to death even though He had never sinned, and He rose again to prove death was defeated. **Jesus' resurrection gives us hope for eternal life**.

Tell the Bible story (10 minutes)

Open your Bible to Matthew 4; Mark 1; Luke 4. Use the Bible storytelling tips on the Bible story page to help you tell the story, or show the Bible story video "Jesus' Temptation."

· Bibles
· "Jesus' Temptation" video
· Big Picture Question Poster
· Bible Story Picture Poster
· Story Point Poster

LEADER • Here is a tricky question for you: Why would it have been sin to make bread? [*Allow responses.*]

It is not usually sin to make bread, but the devil wanted Jesus to stop obeying God. Jesus was in the wilderness without food because that is what God's Spirit told Jesus to do. If Jesus had chosen to use His power to make stones into bread, He would have been disobeying God. Jesus never used His power to satisfy His human desires. He used His power only to glorify God.

Each time Jesus obeyed God, He used a Bible passage to resist the devil's tricks. But did you notice what the devil did the second time he tried to make Jesus sin? The devil tried to twist Scripture to make it seem like something sinful was not sinful. Thankfully, Jesus is more powerful than all the forces of evil. God's plans never fail, and Jesus saw right through the devil's lie.

Jesus resisted all three of the devil's attempts. **Jesus was tempted and never sinned**. He remained perfect, just like He had always been and always will be. So when the time came for Jesus to obey God by dying on the cross, He was the perfect sacrifice just as God planned. Because Jesus died on the cross for us and rose again, we can gain the power we need to resist the devil too.

Christ connection

Note: You may use this opportunity to use Scripture and the guide provided to explain how to become a Christian. Make sure kids know when and where they can ask questions.

LEADER • Everyone who trusts in Jesus is a new creation. God forgives our sin and gives us new hearts that love and want to obey God. God also sends the Holy Spirit to live in us and fill us with His power. We will still be tempted to sin, but with the Holy Spirit we can choose to obey God.

The devil tried to get Jesus to sin, but Jesus never sinned. Jesus always did the right thing. Jesus died on the cross to rescue us from sin. When we are tempted to sin, we can ask Jesus to help us say no to sin.

Questions from kids video (3 minutes)

Show the "Unit 20, Session 2" questions from kids video. Prompt kids to think about times they have been tempted. Guide them to discuss ways we can obey God even when we feel tempted to sin.

· "Unit 20, Session 2" Questions from Kids video

🌐 Missions moment (3 minutes)

Ask a volunteer to read the "Betty Greene Story" printable, or read it yourself if your group lacks strong readers. Display the "Betty Greene Photos" printable or pass them around so kids have a chance to look at them.

· "Betty Greene Photos" printable
· "Betty Greene Story" printable

LEADER • Betty Greene was the first female missionary pilot. She helped to start the Mission Aviation Fellowship (MAF) that uses small airplanes to reach people in remote villages. The MAF helps people and shares the stories of Jesus, like the one we're learning: **Jesus was tempted and never sinned**.

Pray, thanking God for missionaries like Betty Greene and for any missionaries your church supports.

Key passage (5 minutes)

Show the key passage poster. Lead the boys and girls to read together John 3:30. Then sing "He Must Increase but I Must Decrease (John 3:30)."

· Key Passage Poster
· "He Must Increase, but I Must Decrease (John 3:30)" song

LEADER • John the Baptist knew that Jesus is the most important. John wanted his life to glorify Jesus, not himself. That's why he said the words of this verse.

Sing (4 minutes)

· "Jesus Messiah" song

LEADER • Jesus is our Lord and Savior. Though fully God, Jesus became fully human. *Why did Jesus become human? Jesus became human to obey His Father's plan and rescue sinners.* All glory belongs to Him because He is the Messiah.

Sing together "Jesus Messiah."

Pray (2 minutes)

Invite kids to pray before dismissing to apply the story.

LEADER • Father, thank You that **Jesus was tempted and never sinned**. We know that He perfectly understands our suffering and pain but also perfectly obeyed You at all times. Help us love You more and obey You as Jesus did. Give us the wisdom to seek You when we face temptation. Amen.

Dismiss to apply the story

The Gospel: God's Plan for Me

Ask kids if they have ever heard the word *gospel*. Clarify that the word *gospel* means "good news." It is the message about Christ, the kingdom of God, and salvation. Use the following guide to share the gospel with kids.

God rules. Explain to kids that the Bible tells us God created everything, and He is in charge of everything. Invite a volunteer to read Genesis 1:1 from the Bible. Read Revelation 4:11 or Colossians 1:16-17 aloud and explain what these verses mean.

We sinned. Tell kids that since the time of Adam and Eve, everyone has chosen to disobey God. (Romans 3:23) The Bible calls this sin. Because God is holy, God cannot be around sin. Sin separates us from God and deserves God's punishment of death. (Romans 6:23)

God provided. Choose a child to read John 3:16 aloud. Say that God sent His Son, Jesus, the perfect solution to our sin problem, to rescue us from the punishment we deserve. It's something we, as sinners, could never earn on our own. Jesus alone saves us. Read and explain Ephesians 2:8-9.

Jesus gives. Share with kids that Jesus lived a perfect life, died on the cross for our sins, and rose again. Because Jesus gave up His life for us, we can be welcomed into God's family for eternity. This is the best gift ever! Read Romans 5:8; 2 Corinthians 5:21; or 1 Peter 3:18.

We respond. Tell kids that they can respond to Jesus. Read Romans 10:9-10,13. Review these aspects of our response: Believe in your heart that Jesus alone saves you through what He's already done on the cross. Repent, turning from self and sin to Jesus. Tell God and others that your faith is in Jesus.

Offer to talk with any child who is interested in responding to Jesus. Provide *I'm a Christian Now!* for new Christians to take home and complete with their families.

APPLY the Story

SESSION TITLE: Jesus' Temptation

BIBLE PASSAGE: Matthew 4; Mark 1; Luke 4

STORY POINT: Jesus was tempted and never sinned.

KEY PASSAGE: John 3:30

BIG PICTURE QUESTION: Why did Jesus become human? Jesus became human to obey His Father's plan and rescue sinners.

Key passage activity (5 minutes)

· Key Passage Poster
· sticky notes

Read the key passage with the kids. Use sticky notes to cover the a word or two of the key passage. Challenge the kids to say it again, adding in the missing words. Repeat this process until the whole passage is covered and kids say it from memory.

SAY • John wanted his life to bring Jesus glory. John knew that Jesus is the most important person of all. We can also give Jesus glory when we love and obey Him. **Jesus was tempted and never sinned**, so when we are tempted we can ask Jesus for help to obey Him. That's a great way to glorify Jesus.

Discussion & Bible skills (10 minutes)

· Bibles, 1 per kid
· Story Point Poster
· Small Group Timeline and Map Set
(005802970, optional)

Distribute a Bible to each kid. Help them find Mathew 4; Mark 1; Luke 4. Ask a kid to tell you which division those books are in. (*New Testament, Gospels*) Ask another kid to tell you which other book is part of that same division. (*John*) Then ask a third kid to briefly explain what that division contains. (*the stories of Jesus' life and ministry, as well as His death and resurrection*) Consider showing Jerusalem on the New Testament Israel Map. (*H5*)

Ask the following questions. Lead the group to discuss:

Option: Retell or review the Bible story using the bolded text of the Bible story script.

1. Why was Jesus in the wilderness? (*The Spirit sent Him there to pray, fast, and be tempted by Satan; Mark 1:13; Matt. 4:1-2*)

2. What did Satan tempt Jesus to do? (*turn stones to bread, jump off the temple, and worship Satan to get riches and power; Matt. 4:3,6,9*)

3. How did Jesus fight against temptation? (*Jesus quoted Scripture to remember what is true; Matt. 4:4,7,10*)

4. Why do we face temptations? *Guide kids to think about why Satan wants people to sin. Remind them that Satan wants to prevent people from glorifying God and keep Christians from living the way God has commanded us to live. We also have sin natures that desire sin and selfishness. We are tempted when we dwell on sinfulness and when Satan tries to get us to disobey.*

5. Can we resist temptation? *Discuss the difference between people who trust in Jesus and people who do not. Help kids see without Jesus, we cannot avoid sin. Remind them, though, that everyone who trusts in Jesus has the Holy Spirit living inside. Christians can use the power of the Spirit and the Word of God to fight temptation and obey God.*

6. Why is it important to resist temptation? *Help kids see that Christians cannot lose their salvation when they choose sin, but sin still dishonors God, hurts us, and hurts those around us. We resist temptation not to earn God's love, but because we love and trust God that His commands are good for us.*

SAY • **Jesus was tempted and never sinned**. When we face temptation, we can resist it through the Holy Spirit's power and the Word of God.

Activity choice (10 minutes)

 OPTION 1: Now boarding

Arrange chairs into columns with an aisle between. Ensure you have enough chairs for each kid to have a seat. Instruct the kids to sit in the chairs and imagine they are flying in a plane. Stand at the front of the group and call out commands. Kids will react differently depending on which command you give. Use the suggested commands and actions below, or make up your own.

Suggested commands:
- Nose dive: All the kids lean forward.
- Gaining altitude: All the kids lean back.
- Seatbelts fastened: Kids pretend to buckle a lap belt.
- Move about the cabin: Each kid gets up and swaps seats with another kid.
- Turbulence: Kids shake their body around.
- Crash landing: Kids hug their knees and pretend to fall from their chairs.

Tip: Use this activity option to reinforce the missions moment found in Teach the Story.

SAY • That was a fun game. Real pilots may have to deal with all kinds of situations similar to the ones we acted out. Pray for missionary pilots like the ones with MAF. They can reach people in mountain villages, deep jungles, or remote islands that no one else can get to. Their willingness to serve God means that people will be helped and will hear about Jesus. The next time we fly a paper airplane, see an airplane in the sky, or fly in an airplane ourselves, let's say a prayer for missionary pilots.

Pray for the MAF pilots and for any missionaries your church supports. Ask parents or church members to donate travel-size toiletry items for a mission project included in Session 3 of Unit 20.

OPTION 2: Remembrance rocks

Provide each kid a medium-sized rock. Allow the kids to take turns using permanent markers to write the story point or a favorite Bible verse reference on the stones. You may provide decoupage paste and foam brushes for kids to coat their rocks to protect the writing.

· medium-sized rocks
· permanent markers
· decoupage paste and foam brushes (optional)

SAY • The devil tried to convince Jesus to put His human needs before His obedience to God. **Jesus was tempted and never sinned.** Instead of turning stones into bread to eat, Jesus used God's Word to defeat the devil. These remembrance rocks can help us remember to fight temptation so we can glorify Jesus with our lives.

Reflection and prayer (5 minutes)

Distribute a sheet of paper to each child. Ask the kids to write about or draw a picture to answer the following questions:

· pencils and crayons
· paper
· Bible Story Coloring Page, 1 per kid

- What does this story teach me about God or about the gospel?
- What does this story teach me about myself?
- Whom can I tell about this story?

Make sure to send the sheets home with kids alongside the activity page so that parents can see what their kids have been learning.

If time remains, take prayer requests or allow kids to complete the Bible story coloring page provided with this session. Pray for your group.

Tip: Give parents this week's *Big Picture Cards for Families* to allow families to interact with the biblical content at home.

Unit 20 • Session 3
John Pointed to Jesus

BIBLE PASSAGE:
Matthew 3; John 1; 3

STORY POINT:
John the Baptist told people to follow Jesus.

KEY PASSAGE:
John 3:30

BIG PICTURE QUESTION:
Why did Jesus become human? Jesus became human to obey His Father's plan and rescue sinners.

INTRODUCE THE STORY
(10–15 MINUTES)
PAGE 134

→

TEACH THE STORY
(25–30 MINUTES)
PAGE 136

→

APPLY THE STORY
(25–30 MINUTES)
PAGE 142

Additional resources are available at gospelproject.com. For free training and session-by-session help, visit MinistryGrid.com/thegospelproject.

LEADER Bible Study

Hundreds of years before Jesus was born, the prophets had spoken of a forerunner—someone who would get people ready for Jesus. (Isa. 40:3; Mal. 3:1) At just the right time, "John came baptizing in the wilderness and proclaiming a baptism of repentance for the forgiveness of sins" (Mark 1:4). These baptisms were an outward sign of cleansing for people who had repented of their sins.

John's followers were concerned when they saw Jesus and His disciples, who were baptizing people too. They came to John, who pointed out several things about himself and about Jesus. Consider these comparisons as John explained that Jesus was greater than John.

First, who were they? John was clear: "I am not the Messiah" (John 3:28). John was not the bridegroom, but the groom's friend. Jesus is the bridegroom. (John 3:29)

Where did they come from? John was from the earth, and he belonged to the earth. Jesus comes from above and is above all. (John 3:31)

What did they do? John said, "He must increase, but I must decrease." John was a witness to the Light. (John 1:7-8) He was a voice in the wilderness, and Jesus is the Word. (John 1:14,23) John the Baptist told people to get ready for the Messiah. He baptized with water, but Jesus baptized with the Spirit. (John 1:33)

Finally, why were they here? John went before Jesus and rejoiced with Him. (John 3:28-29) Jesus came to give eternal life. (John 3:36)

John described his joy as being complete. (John 3:29) The One for whom he had prepared the people was here. The time had come for John to step aside and let Jesus take the spotlight. John's mission was complete.

The BIBLE Story

John Pointed to Jesus
Matthew 3; John 1; 3

Jesus and His disciples went out into the countryside. People came to see them, and Jesus taught the people. Many people were baptized.

Nearby, John the Baptist was baptizing people too. Some of the people who followed John got into an argument. They **went to John.** "Teacher," they said, "remember the man you talked about, the One who was with you on the other side of the Jordan River? His disciples are baptizing people, and people are starting to follow Him." John's followers were talking about Jesus. John answered them, "You heard me say that I am not the Messiah. I am the messenger who goes before Him to announce that He is coming." This was true. John had said, "Someone greater than me is coming. I am not worthy to remove His sandals. I baptize you with water, but He will baptize you with the Holy Spirit." John tried to explain by talking about a wedding. When two people get married, the man who marries the bride is the groom. His friend stands with him at the wedding, and he is happy to be there and hear the groom's voice. John also knew that a wedding is the groom's special day; **the groom's friend should not make it about himself. This was how John felt—like a groom's friend—because he was happy that Jesus, the Messiah, had come. John said, "Jesus must increase, but I must decrease."**

Then John explained why Jesus was more important than himself. John was from the earth, and he could only talk about things on earth. Jesus—the One who comes from heaven—talked about things in heaven because He had seen them! Still, no one believed what Jesus said.

Whoever believes Jesus knows that God tells the truth. God sent Jesus to earth, and Jesus speaks God's words.

The Father loves the Son and has given Him power over everything. Whoever believes in the Son will have eternal life, but whoever refuses to believe in the Son will not have eternal life. He will never be able to get away from God's judgment.

Christ Connection: John the Baptist told people to get ready for Jesus, the promised Messiah. Now that Jesus was on earth, John's mission was complete. Jesus was greater than John, and John joyfully stepped aside as Jesus began His earthly ministry.

Bible Storytelling Tips

- **Use sound effects:** Play sound effects of a river as you tell the story.
- **Make a T-chart:** List words John used to describe himself and Jesus (*not the Messiah/Messiah, groom's friend/groom*, and so on).

INTRODUCE the Story

SESSION TITLE: John Pointed to Jesus
BIBLE PASSAGE: Matthew 3; John 1; 3
STORY POINT: John the Baptist told people to follow Jesus.
KEY PASSAGE: John 3:30
BIG PICTURE QUESTION: Why did Jesus become human? Jesus became human to obey His Father's plan and rescue sinners.

Welcome time

Greet each kid as he or she arrives. Use this time to collect the offering, fill out attendance sheets, and help new kids connect to your group. Prompt kids to discuss what the word *witness* means. (*to see something happen; a person who can speak with knowledge about something that he has seen happen*)

SAY • The word *witness* probably comes up most often in courtrooms, both real and fictional. A witness is a person who can explain what he saw or heard to help prove whether something is true. We also use the word *witness* to describe our ability to tell other people about what Jesus has done in our lives.

Activity page (5 minutes)

· "Greatest to Least" activity page, 1 per kid
· pencils or markers

Invite kids to complete the "Greatest to Least" activity page. Kids will number the different pictures in order according to which items they value most.

SAY • We all have different opinions on how much we value different things, but I hope we can all agree that Jesus is the most important and valuable of all. Today we will learn about a time John assured people of that.

Session starter (10 minutes)

OPTION 1: Increase or decrease?

Select a kid to think of a number between 1 and 100, including both 1 and 100. Instruct that kid to whisper the number to you, and then allow the other kids to guess the number. After each guess, the kid who's thinking of the number will tell the kids if they should increase or decrease their next guess to be closer. When the kids guess the right number, select a new kid and start again. Be prepared to help kids answer if they are unsure if a guess is above or below their number.

SAY • You had to increase or decrease the values of your guesses to get to the correct answer. Today we will learn about a time John told people that Jesus must increase while he decreased. What do you think it means for Jesus to increase?

OPTION 2: Grow and shrink

Help the kids form pairs. Provide each pair with a stretchy coiled spring toy. Give the pairs a few minutes to play with the toys, encouraging them to stretch them and allow them to retract. Show the kids how to send vibrations or waves along the length of the stretched toy. If you have access to a stairway, consider showing the kids how the toys can "walk" down the stairs by flopping and stretching and coming back together.

· stretchy coiled spring toys, 1 per 2 kids

SAY • Those toys are especially fun because of the ways they can grow and shrink. Today we will learn about John the Baptist. He wanted to "shrink" and Jesus to "grow." We'll learn what that means soon.

Transition to teach the story

TEACH the Story

SESSION TITLE: John Pointed to Jesus

BIBLE PASSAGE: Matthew 3; John 1; 3

STORY POINT: John the Baptist told people to follow Jesus.

KEY PASSAGE: John 3:30

BIG PICTURE QUESTION: Why did Jesus become human? Jesus became human to obey His Father's plan and rescue sinners.

Countdown

· countdown video

Show the countdown video as you transition to teach the story. Set it to end as the session begins.

Introduce the session (3 minutes)

· leader attire
· reflective vest
· hard hat

Tip: If you prefer not to use themed content or characters, adapt or omit this introduction.

[Leader enters wearing blue jeans, a T-shirt with a reflective vest, and a hard hat.]

LEADER • Hi there! Good to see you again. We're pretty close to finishing our road work. In fact, we've got one lane open again. As you can imagine, one lane of traffic isn't enough since cars need to go in both directions. For now, I've been directing traffic with a sign that stops people from one direction and instructs the people from the other direction to drive slowly. Every few minutes, I switch it around so the stopped cars have a chance to go too.

Sometimes I wonder what would happen if people got so used to following my sign that they did not know what to do when the road is finished and the permanent signs are up. It would cause a lot of problems. You see, my job as a traffic director is temporary. Once the road is done, people should look to the real signs and markings on the pavement and follow those. In a way, it reminds me of another story about John the Baptist and Jesus. John spent some time teaching and leading people, but it was time for him to step aside so Jesus—the fully God, fully human Messiah—could lead His people.

Big picture question (1 minute)

LEADER • Jesus is God the Son, and it is important to understand why God the Son came to earth as a human. That's our big picture question! *Why did Jesus become human? Jesus became human to obey His Father's plan and rescue sinners.* God's perfect plan to rescue sinners required Jesus to be a human to be the perfect sacrifice for sin. Jesus wanted to obey this plan because He loves God and He loves people.

Giant timeline (1 minute)

Show the giant timeline. Point to individual Bible stories as you review.

· Giant Timeline

LEADER • You may remember a few weeks back. We learned that **Jesus obeyed God by being baptized.** God announced His love for Jesus, and the Holy Spirit landed on Jesus like a dove. The Holy Spirit led Jesus into the wilderness where Satan tried to trick Jesus and make Him sin. **Jesus was tempted and never sinned**. He remained perfect and able to be the perfect sacrifice. Today, we will learn about what John the Baptist taught about Jesus when Jesus began traveling around teaching, healing, and baptizing people.

Tell the Bible story (10 minutes)

· Bibles
· "John Pointed to Jesus" video
· Big Picture Question Poster
· Bible Story Picture Poster
· Story Point Poster

Open your Bible to Matthew 3; John 1; 3. Use the Bible storytelling tips on the Bible story page to help you tell the story, or show the Bible story video "John Pointed to Jesus."

LEADER • You probably recognized a lot of this story because of our key passage. John understood that Jesus is the most important. John wanted those who were following him to understand that too.

John the Baptist told people to follow Jesus. John spoke about a wedding. If you go to a wedding, you celebrate the man and woman getting married. In a way, it's also like a birthday party. When you go to a friend's party, you know that people are celebrating the birthday girl, not you. John was ready to step aside so Jesus could get the glory He deserves. John wanted people to celebrate and obey Jesus.

How can we celebrate Jesus in our lives? [*Allow responses.*] Those are great ideas! We can sing praise songs to Jesus, talk to Him, tell others about Him, and give Him the glory in everything we do. We can obey God's commands, such as loving our neighbors, praying for our enemies, honoring our parents, or being baptized when we believe in Jesus. All of these are different and effective ways to celebrate and worship Jesus.

Christ connection

Note: You may use this opportunity to use Scripture and the guide provided to explain how to become a Christian. Make sure kids know when and where they can ask questions.

LEADER • John the Baptist told people to get ready for Jesus, the promised Messiah. Now that Jesus was on earth, John's mission was complete. Jesus was greater than John, and John joyfully stepped aside as Jesus began His earthly ministry.

138

Questions from kids video (3 minutes)

Show the "Unit 20, Session 3" questions from kids video. Prompt kids to think about fame and wealth. Guide them to discuss reasons God's glory is more important than our own fame or wealth.

· "Unit 20, Session 3" Questions from Kids video

Missions moment (3 minutes)

Display the "Thiemann Family Photo" printable. Ask a volunteer to read the caption, or read it aloud for kids to hear.

· "Thiemann Family Photo" printable

LEADER • The Thiemanns live in Lesotho (leh-SOO-too), a small country in southern Africa. Jason Thiemann is a pilot and mechanic with Mission Aviation Fellowship. Life in Lesotho isn't always easy, but the Thiemanns are there to be obedient to Jesus and to share the gospel. **John the Baptist told people to follow Jesus.** That's what missionaries do, too.

Key passage (5 minutes)

Show the key passage poster. Lead the boys and girls to read together John 3:30. Then sing "He Must Increase, but I Must Decrease (John 3:30)."

· Key Passage Poster
· "He Must Increase, but I Must Decrease (John 3:30)" song

LEADER • Our key passage comes directly from the story we learned about today! John did not want people to argue whether John or Jesus was more important. John knew the answer is Jesus. John wanted everyone else to know that, too. **John the Baptist told people to follow Jesus.** He said that he must decrease and Jesus must increase.

Sing (4 minutes)

LEADER • John understood what we are learning. Jesus is

· "Take It to the Lord" song

the most important. Jesus deserves all glory because He is God's Son, born as a human to rescue us. He's the best friend we could have, and we can take all our worries to Him.

Sing together "Take It to the Lord."

Pray (2 minutes)

Invite kids to pray before dismissing to apply the story.

LEADER • Father, help us show the same humility that John showed. Help us understand that Jesus is the only One who deserves glory. Give us opportunities to celebrate and obey Him. We ask You to decrease our pride and increase Jesus' glory through our lives. Amen.

Dismiss to apply the story

The Gospel: God's Plan for Me

Ask kids if they have ever heard the word *gospel*. Clarify that the word *gospel* means "good news." It is the message about Christ, the kingdom of God, and salvation. Use the following guide to share the gospel with kids.

God rules. Explain to kids that the Bible tells us God created everything, and He is in charge of everything. Invite a volunteer to read Genesis 1:1 from the Bible. Read Revelation 4:11 or Colossians 1:16-17 aloud and explain what these verses mean.

We sinned. Tell kids that since the time of Adam and Eve, everyone has chosen to disobey God. (Romans 3:23) The Bible calls this sin. Because God is holy, God cannot be around sin. Sin separates us from God and deserves God's punishment of death. (Romans 6:23)

God provided. Choose a child to read John 3:16 aloud. Say that God sent His Son, Jesus, the perfect solution to our sin problem, to rescue us from the punishment we deserve. It's something we, as sinners, could never earn on our own. Jesus alone saves us. Read and explain Ephesians 2:8-9.

Jesus gives. Share with kids that Jesus lived a perfect life, died on the cross for our sins, and rose again. Because Jesus gave up His life for us, we can be welcomed into God's family for eternity. This is the best gift ever! Read Romans 5:8; 2 Corinthians 5:21; or 1 Peter 3:18.

We respond. Tell kids that they can respond to Jesus. Read Romans 10:9-10,13. Review these aspects of our response: Believe in your heart that Jesus alone saves you through what He's already done on the cross. Repent, turning from self and sin to Jesus. Tell God and others that your faith is in Jesus.

Offer to talk with any child who is interested in responding to Jesus. Provide *I'm a Christian Now!* for new Christians to take home and complete with their families.

APPLY the Story

SESSION TITLE: John Pointed to Jesus

BIBLE PASSAGE: Matthew 3; John 1; 3

STORY POINT: John the Baptist told people to follow Jesus.

KEY PASSAGE: John 3:30

BIG PICTURE QUESTION: Why did Jesus become human? Jesus became human to obey His Father's plan and rescue sinners.

Key passage activity (5 minutes)

· Key Passage Poster
· marker
· index cards

Write each word of the key passage on a separate index card. Make enough sets of index cards so that every pair of kids will have one set. Form pairs of kids to play a matching game. Kids will take turns flipping two cards face up. If the words are next to one another, such as *must* and *increase*, the kid who flipped them over may keep the pair. If not he must flip them back. If there are any unmatchable cards left at the end of the game, allow the kids to flip them over to end the game. After the game ends, pairs will work together to arrange all the cards in order. Then allow volunteers to say the passage from memory.

SAY • John wanted everyone to glorify Jesus. That's why **John the Baptist told people to follow Jesus**. In our own lives, we can increase Jesus' glory by loving Him, obeying Him, and loving others.

Discussion & Bible skills (10 minutes)

· Bibles, 1 per kid
· Story Point Poster
· Small Group Timeline and Map Set (005802970, optional)

Distribute a Bible to each kid. Help kids find John 3. Select a strong reader to read verses 27-30. Explain the purpose of Bible divisions (*to help us organize and understand what God's Word teaches*) and say the division John is in. (*Gospels*)

Ask the following questions. Lead the group to discuss:

Option: Retell or review the Bible story using the bolded text of the Bible story script.

1. What were Jesus and His disciples doing in the countryside? (*teaching and baptizing people, John 3:22*)

2. Why were John's disciples arguing? (*Many were starting to follow Jesus instead of John, John 3:26*)

3. What did John want to happen? (*John wanted Jesus to get the glory as Messiah; John 3:30-31,35*)

4. Why is it good to glorify Jesus? *Guide kids to understand that people were created by God to glorify God. Jesus is God the Son. When we glorify Him in our lives, we are fulfilling our purpose, and it is good for us. Everything God does is for His glory and our good, including creating us to worship Him.*

5. When is it hard to glorify Jesus? *Discuss situations kids may face that can fill them with pride or arrogance. Explain that sinful pride makes it impossible to glorify Jesus. Remind them that our gifts and talents were given by God as a way to glorify God. When we do well, we can thank God and remind other people about His goodness to bless us with talents or skills.*

6. How can we learn to show humility? *Explain that the first step toward humility is understanding who Jesus is. He is God's beloved Son. He is the Messiah. The story of our lives is ultimately about Him, not any of us. Help kids consider that all people are equally valuable to God as all people are made in His image. None of us are better. All of us are His creations.*

SAY • **John the Baptist told people to follow Jesus.** John wanted people to make Jesus the center of their lives. When we love and trust Jesus, we will want to obey and glorify Him above all things.

Prepare the Way

assorted travel-size toiletry items (toothpaste, toothbrushes, deodorant, shampoo, body wash, and so forth)
- quart-size ziplock bags
- index cards
- crayons and markers

Tip: Use this activity option to reinforce the missions moment found in Teach the Story.

Activity choice (10 minutes)

OPTION 1: Travel kits for missions

Gather an assortment of donated travel-size toiletry items. Invite kids to assemble travel kits by putting one of each kind of item into a quart-sized ziplock bag. Ask kids to include a short encouraging note or draw a picture on an index card. Put one decorated index card in each bag. Arrange a time to give these bags to members of your church who are going on short-term missions trips, or donate them to a church in your area that is leading a short-term trip.

SAY • Sometimes, missionaries will go for just a short trip, maybe a week or so. One way we can support them is to make some kits to make traveling long distances a bit easier. You don't have to travel on a mission trip to live on mission!

LOW PREP

OPTION 2: Alphabet praises

Direct the kids to sit in a circle. Select a kid to start the game by saying a trait of Jesus or a reason why He deserves all glory. This word must start with the letter *A*. The kid to her right will say another trait or reason, starting with the letter *B* this time. Play continues in this way until a trait has been named for every letter of the alphabet. Be prepared with some ideas of words for trickier letters, such as *Q* or *X*, and consider allowing some flexible rules, such as using words that start with *Ex-* instead of *X*.

SAY • Jesus is the greatest of all. We love and praise Him because He alone is the perfect Messiah who died to save us from sin. **John the Baptist told people to follow Jesus**. We can tell others to follow Jesus as well!

Reflection and prayer (5 minutes)

Distribute a sheet of paper to each child. Ask the kids to write about or draw a picture to answer the following questions:

- What does this story teach me about God or about the gospel?
- What does this story teach me about myself?
- Whom can I tell about this story?

Make sure to send the sheets home with kids alongside the activity page so that parents can see what their kids have been learning.

If time remains, take prayer requests or allow kids to complete the Bible story coloring page provided with this session. Pray for your group.

· pencils and crayons
· paper
· Bible Story Coloring Page, 1 per kid

Tip: Give parents this week's *Big Picture Cards for Families* to allow families to interact with the biblical content at home.

Use Week of:

Unit 20 · Session 4
Jesus Called Disciples

BIBLE PASSAGE:
Matthew 4; 9; Mark 1–3;
Luke 5–6

STORY POINT:
Jesus called disciples to follow Him.

KEY PASSAGE:
John 3:30

BIG PICTURE QUESTION:
Why did Jesus become human? Jesus
became human to obey His Father's
plan and rescue sinners.

INTRODUCE THE STORY
(10–15 MINUTES)
PAGE 150

→

TEACH THE STORY
(25–30 MINUTES)
PAGE 152

→

APPLY THE STORY
(25–30 MINUTES)
PAGE 158

Additional resources are available at gospelproject.com. For free training and
session-by-session help, visit MinistryGrid.com/thegospelproject.

LEADER Bible Study

In the first century, *rabbi* was a title given to a respected expert in the law of Moses. A rabbi studied the Scriptures and taught through speaking and writing. Jews wanted to honor God in how they lived, and they looked to the rabbis to instruct them in their behavior.

The word *rabbi* translates "my master." Jewish students would seek out a rabbi and ask to follow him. A rabbi would choose only a few highly-promising students to be his disciples. If a student was not accepted by the rabbi, he likely returned home to learn a trade. Those chosen to be a rabbi's disciples followed him everywhere. They learned from the rabbi how to think and how to act. They trusted the rabbi, and the goal was to become just like him.

When Jesus chose His disciples, His strategy was unusual. Rather than waiting for students to come to Him, Jesus sought out His disciples among the people who followed Him. He found them working—fishing and repairing nets. Some of Jesus' disciples were introduced to Him by their friends. He approached these ordinary men and said, "Follow Me." Their response? "Immediately they left ... and followed him" (Matt. 4:20,22).

The Twelve—Simon (Peter) and his brother Andrew; James and John; Philip; Bartholomew; Matthew; Thomas; James, son of Alphaeus; Thaddaeus; Simon; and Judas—spent time with Jesus during His ministry. Jesus taught them how to live in light of God's coming kingdom. He commissioned them to teach others about Him. The good news about Jesus is too great to not share with the entire world.

The call to follow Jesus is not an easy one. Jesus said, "If anyone wants to follow after me, let him deny himself, take up his cross, and follow me" (Matt. 16:24). Jesus calls us to do the same—to surrender our lives for His purposes and perhaps even to die. "For whoever wants to save his life will lose it, but whoever loses his life because of me will find it" (Matt. 16:25)

The **BIBLE** Story

Jesus Called Disciples

Matthew 4; 9; Mark 1–3; Luke 5–6

Jesus' ministry had begun. He traveled around, preaching about God and telling people to turn away from their sins. People started talking about Jesus and the things He was teaching. They were interested in what Jesus had to say. **Large crowds followed Jesus around and listened to Him teach.**

One day, Jesus was walking along the Sea of Galilee. He saw two brothers: Simon—who was called Peter—and Andrew. Peter and Andrew were fishermen. **Jesus called out to them, "Follow Me, and I will teach you to fish for people!" Right away, Peter and Andrew dropped their nets and followed Jesus.**

Later, He saw two more brothers. Their names were James and John. They were in a boat fixing nets with their father, Zebedee. **Jesus called out to them, and right away they got up, left their father and the boat, and followed Jesus.**

Jesus went on and saw a man named **Matthew** (who was also called Levi). Matthew was sitting at the tax office. Matthew was a tax collector. Many people didn't like tax collectors because tax collectors were unfair. **Jesus called out to him, "Follow Me!" So Matthew got up, left everything behind, and** followed Jesus.

Matthew had a big feast for Jesus at his house. Many tax collectors and sinners came to eat with Jesus and His disciples. The religious leaders saw this, and they didn't think Jesus should be friends with people who did wrong things. They complained to the disciples, "Why does your Teacher eat and drink with tax collectors and sinners?"

Jesus heard the religious leaders and said, "People who are healthy don't need a doctor, but people who are sick do. I did not come to invite good people; I came to invite sinners to turn back to God."

Later, Jesus gathered His followers together and chose twelve of them to be His apostles. Jesus' apostles would work closely with Jesus and would go out to tell others about Him. These are the men Jesus chose: Simon (who was called Peter), Simon's brother Andrew, James and John (who were called the "Sons of Thunder"), Philip and Bartholomew, Matthew and Thomas, James the son of Alphaeus (al FEE uhs), Thaddaeus (THAD ih uhs), Simon the Zealot, and Judas Iscariot (iss KAR ih aht).

Christ Connection: Jesus came to earth to show what God is like and to save people from their sins. This is great news! Jesus told His disciples to tell others about Him, and we are Jesus' disciples when we trust in Him. Everyone in the world needs to hear the good news about Jesus.

Bible Storytelling Tips

• **List names:** Write the disciples' names on a dry erase board and point to them as you tell the story.
• **Use props:** Display fishing nets as you tell about the fishermen who left their nets to follow Jesus.

INTRODUCE the Story

SESSION TITLE: Jesus Called Disciples
BIBLE PASSAGE: Matthew 4; 9; Mark 1–3; Luke 5–6
STORY POINT: Jesus called disciples to follow Him.
KEY PASSAGE: John 3:30
BIG PICTURE QUESTION: Why did Jesus become human? Jesus became human to obey His Father's plan and rescue sinners.

Welcome time

Note: Be sensitive to kids who may struggle to make friends.

Greet each kid as he or she arrives. Use this time to collect the offering, fill out attendance sheets, and help new kids connect to your group. Prompt kids to tell about their closest friends.

SAY • Having friends is a great blessing from the Lord. It can be difficult to maintain close friendships with many people, so we often have a smaller group of very close friends. Today we will hear about when Jesus chose some people to be His closest friends and followers.

Activity page (5 minutes)

· "A Change of Pace" activity page, 1 per kid
· pencils or markers

Invite kids to complete the "A Change of Pace" activity page. Direct kids to find and circle the seven differences between the two versions of the Bible story art.

SAY • Great job finding those changes. When Jesus came and called His disciples to follow Him, they were in for a drastic change to their lives. Everyone who follows Jesus experiences incredible life changes. I'll tell you more about that soon.

Session starter (10 minutes)

LOW PREP

OPTION 1: Follow the leader

Instruct the kids to stand in a single-file line. Select a kid to lead the line around the room. She may do various motions or move in silly ways. The rest of the kids in line must mimic her motions and movements. After a minute or so, select a new kid to lead the line. Play as time allows.

SAY • Today we will learn about Jesus' disciples. *Disciples* are people who follow someone else. Jesus' disciples followed Him, learned to obey Him, and were His closest friends. Who would you choose to be your followers and friends?

OPTION 2: Boats in the water

Provide each kid with a sheet of aluminum foil. Help the kids to form their foil sheets into boat shapes. Provide a basin of water and allow the kids to see if their boats will float. You may use pennies, marbles, or other small weights to see whose boat can hold the most weight before sinking.

- aluminum foil
- basin
- water
- small weights, pennies, or marbles (optional)

SAY • Many of Jesus' disciples were fishermen when Jesus met them. When Jesus called them, they left their boats and followed Jesus immediately. Jesus promised to teach them a new way to fish. What do you think they would catch?

Transition to teach the story

TEACH the Story

SESSION TITLE: Jesus Called Disciples
BIBLE PASSAGE: Matthew 4; 9; Mark 1–3; Luke 5–6
STORY POINT: Jesus called disciples to follow Him.
KEY PASSAGE: John 3:30
BIG PICTURE QUESTION: Why did Jesus become human? Jesus became human to obey His Father's plan and rescue sinners.

Countdown

· countdown video

Show the countdown video as you transition to teach the story. Set it to end as the session begins.

Introduce the session (3 minutes)

· leader attire
· reflective vest
· hard hat

Tip: If you prefer not to use themed content or characters, adapt or omit this introduction.

[Leader enters wearing blue jeans, a T-shirt with a reflective vest, and a hard hat.]

LEADER • Hey, everyone! The road work on this portion of the highway is complete. Everything about the road is improved. There are more lanes to drive in, no potholes to avoid, and much clearer signs and markings to direct people where to go.

I'll tell you one thing I've never experienced before: the road is done, but no one is using it! I guess people got so used to the construction and terrible traffic that they all found different ways to get where they are going. That's why a few friends and I have started a special team. Our job (at least until the next road work assignment) is to wake up each day and drive onto the highway to get around the city. It may seem silly, but our hope is that people will see us driving on the new road and know that it's open again. Then, maybe they will follow us and use the new road like we wanted them to when we fixed it. In other words, they can follow us as we follow the road.

You know, that idea we had actually reminds me of a Bible story. It's about Jesus and the time He chose certain men to be His closest friends and followers.

Big picture question (1 minute)

LEADER • As we get to the story, let's review the big picture question. *Why did Jesus become human? Jesus became human to obey His Father's plan and rescue sinners.* Jesus is God the Son, and He loves God the Father. As a result, Jesus wanted to obey the Father's perfect plan. Jesus also loves people and wants to see us saved from sin. God's plan for Jesus to die on the cross required Jesus to become human. Jesus wanted to obey God and save people, so He perfectly obeyed God's plan.

Giant timeline (1 minute)

Show the giant timeline. Point to individual Bible stories as you review.

· Giant Timeline

LEADER • Jesus obeyed all aspects of God's plan. **Jesus obeyed God by being baptized.** Then Jesus obeyed the Holy Spirit and prayed in the wilderness for 40 days without food. **Jesus was tempted and never sinned**. When people who had been following John showed confusion about others following Jesus, **John the Baptist told people to follow Jesus**. This week, we will see that **Jesus called disciples to follow Him**. And that's exactly what the disciples did!

Prepare the Way

Tell the Bible story (10 minutes)

Open your Bible to Matthew 4; 9; Mark 1–3; Luke 5–6. Use the Bible storytelling tips on the Bible story page to help you tell the story, or show the Bible story video "Jesus Called Disciples."

LEADER • Jesus called disciples to follow Him. You know what I find so amazing about this story? The men Jesus called left basically everything they had to follow and obey Jesus. The fishermen walked away from their boats, and the tax collector left his tax booth. When Jesus called, they answered. They were far from perfect, but they obeyed right away. They seemed to know that what they were giving up was nothing compared to what they would gain by following Jesus.

And again, the men Jesus called were not people without sin. Many of the people who followed Jesus sinned in ways that were very obvious. That's one of the big reasons the religious leaders hated Jesus. They thought that the Messiah would only spend time with and love people who were good (or at least looked and acted like they were good).

Jesus knew that if people were righteous—their hearts and actions lined up with God's Word—then He wouldn't have needed to come to earth. But people are not righteous, and God's plan required that Jesus come to earth as a human. *Why did Jesus become human? Jesus became human to obey His Father's plan and rescue sinners.* Just as sick people need a doctor, sinners need Jesus. The religious leaders at the time were like sick people who did not believe they were sick.

Christ connection

LEADER • Jesus came to earth to show what God is like and to save people from their sins. This is great news! Jesus told His disciples to tell others about Him, and we are Jesus' disciples when we trust in Him. Everyone in the world needs to hear the good news about Jesus.

Note: You may use this opportunity to use Scripture and the guide provided to explain how to become a Christian. Make sure kids know when and where they can ask questions.

Questions from kids video (3 minutes)

Show the "Unit 20, Session 4" questions from kids video. Prompt kids to think about when they like, or dislike, God's plan. Guide them to discuss what makes it easy—or hard—to trust God.

· "Unit 20, Session 4" Questions from Kids video

🌐 Missions moment (3 minutes)

Ask for volunteers to read aloud some of the ways that kids can get involved in helping a mission organization like Mission Aviation Fellowship. Specifically look at the prayer list on page 2. Take time together to pray for some of the requests.

· "How Kids Can Help MAF" printable

LEADER • Our prayers for missionaries are very important, and it's important for us to remember that we can be on mission wherever we go. **Jesus called disciples to follow Him.** He calls us today to follow Him, too.

Key passage (5 minutes)

Show the key passage poster. Lead the boys and girls to read together John 3:30. Then sing "He Must Increase, but I Must Decrease (John 3:30)."

· Key Passage Poster
· "He Must Increase, but I Must Decrease (John 3:30)" song

LEADER • When John the Baptist said these words, he was explaining to people who had been following him that it was time to follow Jesus instead. When Jesus

Prepare the Way

called people to follow Him, they left everything to do so. We can follow Jesus too!

Sing (4 minutes)

· "Jesus Messiah" song

LEADER • We follow Jesus because He is the Messiah. He deserves all our praise.

Sing together "Jesus Messiah."

Pray (2 minutes)

Invite kids to pray before dismissing to apply the story.

LEADER • Father, thank You for sending Jesus to rescue us. Help us follow Him each day. Give us love for Jesus and for the people we meet each day. Fill us with Your Spirit so we can obey You more. Amen.

Dismiss to apply the story

The Gospel: God's Plan for Me

Ask kids if they have ever heard the word *gospel*. Clarify that the word *gospel* means "good news." It is the message about Christ, the kingdom of God, and salvation. Use the following guide to share the gospel with kids.

God rules. Explain to kids that the Bible tells us God created everything, and He is in charge of everything. Invite a volunteer to read Genesis 1:1 from the Bible. Read Revelation 4:11 or Colossians 1:16-17 aloud and explain what these verses mean.

We sinned. Tell kids that since the time of Adam and Eve, everyone has chosen to disobey God. (Romans 3:23) The Bible calls this sin. Because God is holy, God cannot be around sin. Sin separates us from God and deserves God's punishment of death. (Romans 6:23)

God provided. Choose a child to read John 3:16 aloud. Say that God sent His Son, Jesus, the perfect solution to our sin problem, to rescue us from the punishment we deserve. It's something we, as sinners, could never earn on our own. Jesus alone saves us. Read and explain Ephesians 2:8-9.

Jesus gives. Share with kids that Jesus lived a perfect life, died on the cross for our sins, and rose again. Because Jesus gave up His life for us, we can be welcomed into God's family for eternity. This is the best gift ever! Read Romans 5:8; 2 Corinthians 5:21; or 1 Peter 3:18.

We respond. Tell kids that they can respond to Jesus. Read Romans 10:9-10,13. Review these aspects of our response: Believe in your heart that Jesus alone saves you through what He's already done on the cross. Repent, turning from self and sin to Jesus. Tell God and others that your faith is in Jesus.

Offer to talk with any child who is interested in responding to Jesus. Provide *I'm a Christian Now!* for new Christians to take home and complete with their families.

APPLY the Story

SESSION TITLE: Jesus Called Disciples

BIBLE PASSAGE: Matthew 4; 9; Mark 1–3; Luke 5–6

STORY POINT: Jesus called disciples to follow Him.

KEY PASSAGE: John 3:30

BIG PICTURE QUESTION: Why did Jesus become human? Jesus became human to obey His Father's plan and rescue sinners.

Key passage activity (5 minutes)

· Key Passage Poster
· marker
· index cards
· paper clips
· magnet
· stick or dowel (optional)
· string

Write each word or phrase of the key passage on a separate index card. Place a paper clip onto the edge of each card. Attach a magnet to the end of a length of string. You may attach the other end of the string to a stick or dowel. Allow the kids to take turns using the magnet and string to try and "catch" the key passage cards. After kids catch all the cards, challenge them to put the cards in order.

SAY • John told people that Jesus is the One they should follow. Today we heard how Jesus called disciples to follow Him. All of us should seek to follow Jesus in a way that glorifies Him and not ourselves.

Discussion & Bible skills (10 minutes)

· Bibles, 1 per kid
· Story Point Poster
· Small Group Timeline and Map Set (005802970, optional)

Distribute a Bible to each kid. Help kids find Matthew 4. You may use the New Testament Israel Map to show the kids where the Sea of Galilee is. (*D6*) Discuss the slightly different accounts found in the gospels. Remind the kids that each gospel is written by a different man, but all their accounts are inspired by God and trustworthy. This is why some of the events in one book may not be in others or are recorded from slightly different perspectives.

Ask the following questions. Lead the group to discuss:

Option: Retell or review the Bible story using the bolded text of the Bible story script.

1. What did Jesus say He would teach His disciples to do? (*fish for people, Matt. 4:19*)
2. What were some things Jesus' disciples left behind to follow Him? (*nets, boats, family, jobs, and so forth; Matt. 4:20-22; 9:9*)
3. With whom did Jesus eat and spend His time? (*sinners and tax collectors, Matt. 9:10*)
4. Why does Jesus love sinners? *Help kids understand that everyone is a sinner, and Jesus loves all people because we are created in God's image. Jesus wants to see people repent of sin, turning to God to be saved. He loves sinners and rescues them. He helps us turn away from sin and glorify God instead.*
5. What might we lose by following Jesus? *Guide kids to talk about the cost of loving and obeying Jesus. Help them think about the ways others might react to them, the influence they may lose, or the persecution they may face. Remind the kids that, in some places, following Jesus may even cost a person her life.*
6. What can we gain by following Jesus? *Discuss the unending joy and eternal life we have with God when we have faith in Jesus. Point kids to the hope they have in life: that we gain new purpose, can resist sin, and are filled with the Holy Spirit's power. Point kids also to the hope we have for the future: that Jesus will return and fix all that sin has broken. On that day, we will reign with Christ as children of God.*

SAY • **Jesus called disciples to follow Him.** If we have faith in Jesus, we are His disciples as well. God forgives us and gives us power to live for Him. That means we can call people to follow Jesus, too!

Tip: Use this activity option to reinforce the missions moment found in Teach the Story.

Activity choice (10 minutes)

OPTION 1: MAF helpers

Provide each kid a copy of the "How Kids Can Help MAF" printable. Allow kids to color the handout and complete the activities. Help younger kids complete the activities together. Ask kids questions about the airplane they like the best or where they might like to fly one day.

SAY • **Jesus called disciples to follow Him**. When we learn about missionaries and how to support them, we are part of God's plan to reach all people with the gospel. No matter your age, you can be on mission by telling people to follow Jesus as His disciples did.

OPTION 2: Discipleship in the real world

Direct the kids to sit in a circle. Teach them a simple trick or new skill. This can be anything: making a paper airplane, tying shoes in a new way, whistling, winking, or any other skill you can teach. Work with the kids to learn the skill and talk to them about what makes the skill easy or hard to learn. Challenge them to teach that skill to a friend or sibling.

SAY • Those new skills were not super important to know, but the way I taught you to do them is a picture of discipleship. **Jesus called disciples to follow Him**. As Christians, we can help to train new Christians to follow Jesus, too. We can show what it looks like to love and obey Jesus in all parts of our lives. By talking to people about the difficulties and joys of obeying Jesus—and showing them what that looks like—we can teach them to do the same.

Reflection and prayer (5 minutes)

Distribute a sheet of paper to each child. Ask the kids to write about or draw a picture to answer the following questions:

- What does this story teach me about God or about the gospel?
- What does this story teach me about myself?
- Whom can I tell about this story?

Make sure to send the sheets home with kids alongside the activity page so that parents can see what their kids have been learning.

If time remains, take prayer requests or allow kids to complete the Bible story coloring page provided with this session. Pray for your group.

- pencils and crayons
- paper
- Bible Story Coloring Page, 1 per kid

Tip: Give parents this week's *Big Picture Cards for Families* to allow families to interact with the biblical content at home.

Unit 21 · Session 1
Jesus' Early Miracles

BIBLE PASSAGE:
Mark 1

STORY POINT:
People came to Jesus, and He healed them.

KEY PASSAGE:
John 3:16

BIG PICTURE QUESTION:
What makes people special? People are special because we are made in God's image, as male and female, to know Him.

INTRODUCE THE STORY (10–15 MINUTES) PAGE 166	**TEACH THE STORY** (25–30 MINUTES) PAGE 168	**APPLY THE STORY** (25–30 MINUTES) PAGE 174

 → →

Additional resources are available at gospelproject.com. For free training and session-by-session help, visit MinistryGrid.com/thegospelproject.

LEADER Bible Study

Early in His ministry, Jesus and His disciples traveled to Capernaum, a town on the northwestern shore of the Sea of Galilee. Capernaum became Jesus' home and headquarters. (See Matt. 4:13.) He entered the synagogue on the Sabbath, when people would gather to hear and learn from the Scriptures.

Jesus quickly set Himself apart from the scribes and other religious teachers. Unlike the scribes, who relied completely on traditional interpretations of the Torah from other teachers, Jesus spoke with authority. His teaching came from His own authority as the Author of truth, and it had a profound effect on His listeners—they were astonished!

The early miracles recorded in Mark 1 demonstrate Jesus' power and authority as the Son of God. Jesus drove an unclean spirit from a man in the synagogue; even the demons obey His commands. Then Jesus healed Peter's mother-in-law, and that evening the people in the town brought to Jesus all those who were sick or afflicted with unclean spirits. What did Jesus do? He healed them! (Mark 1:34)

Jesus' miracles continued, and He healed a man with leprosy. *Leprosy* is a skin disease that would have marked a person as "unclean," requiring him to be separated from the community. Jesus had compassion on the man and healed him immediately.

Jesus' miracles brought many people to faith in Him. They also proved that Jesus is the Messiah, the Son of God. These miracles strengthened people's faith and met their needs. Isaiah prophesied that the promised Messiah would bear our sickness and carry our pain. (Isa. 53:4) Jesus fulfilled this prophecy as He healed people.

Help kids make the connection that through Jesus, God did what is impossible for us to do on our own. He provided forgiveness, salvation, and eternal life for all who would trust in Him.

The **BIBLE** Story

Jesus' Early Miracles
Mark 1

Jesus traveled to Capernaum (kuh PUHR nay uhm) with His disciples Simon, Andrew, James, and John. He **went into the synagogue on the Sabbath and began to teach. The people there were very surprised. Jesus' teaching was not like the scribes' teaching. He spoke with authority.** Just then, a man with an unclean spirit shouted, "What do You have to do with us, Jesus of Nazareth? Have You come to destroy us? I know who You are—the Holy One of God!" Jesus commanded the spirit to be quiet and come out of the man. The spirit yelled again and then came out.

Everyone was amazed! "Who is this Jesus?" they asked. "He teaches with authority, and the unclean spirits obey Him!" News about Jesus spread quickly throughout all of Galilee.

Next, Jesus and His disciples went to Simon and Andrew's house. Simon's mother-in-law was in bed with a fever. Jesus went to her, took her hand, and healed her. She got up and began to serve them. **That evening, large crowds of people came to the house with others who were sick or bothered by evil spirits, and Jesus healed them.**

Early the next morning, Jesus went out by Himself to pray. Simon and the other disciples found Him and said, "Everyone is looking for You."

Jesus said, "Let's go on to the nearby villages so I can preach there too. This is why I have come."

Jesus traveled throughout Galilee. He preached and drove out demons. A man with a skin disease came to Jesus. He got on his knees and begged: "If You are willing, You can make me clean." Jesus was willing, and He healed the man.

Christ Connection: Jesus' miracles proved that Jesus is the Messiah, the Son of God. They strengthened people's faith and met their needs. Through Jesus, God did what is impossible for us to do on our own. He provided forgiveness, salvation, and eternal life.

Bible Storytelling Tips

• **Change pace:** Draw attention to dialogue by slowing your pace slightly when speaking dialogue.
• **Pause for effect:** Use pauses and silence between paragraphs to capture kids' attention.

INTRODUCE the Story

SESSION TITLE: Jesus' Early Miracles
BIBLE PASSAGE: Mark 1
STORY POINT: People came to Jesus, and He healed them.
KEY PASSAGE: John 3:16
BIG PICTURE QUESTION: What makes people special? People are special because we are made in God's image, as male and female, to know Him.

Welcome time

Greet each kid as he or she arrives. Use this time to collect the offering, fill out attendance sheets, and help new kids connect to your group. Prompt kids to discuss ways they can help others.

SAY • Those are some great ideas about helping others. When we help other people, it shows them that we love them. Today we will learn about some of the people Jesus helped in the beginning part of His ministry on earth.

Activity page (5 minutes)

· "Helpers Gonna Help" activity page, 1 per kid
· pencils or markers

Invite kids to complete the "Helpers Gonna Help" activity page. Ask kids to match each helper with the one who needs help. Discuss different ways people help one another.

SAY • Some jobs are all about helping people. Doctors help people get well, teachers help people learn, and moms and dads help kids in a million ways. Today we will talk about the greatest help people could ever receive. Jesus came to save us from sin. How else did Jesus help people?

Session starter (10 minutes)

OPTION 1: Listen, watch, follow

Instruct the kids to stand on one side of the room. Stand opposite them and instruct them to mimic your movements and obey your commands. Begin making simple movements, such as waving a hand, patting your belly, or standing on one foot. Sprinkle in spoken commands, telling the kids to do something you are not doing.

SAY • It was a little bit difficult to follow both my words and my actions, especially when I wasn't doing what I said. You had to listen carefully and watch closely. Today we will learn about some things Jesus did that caused people to listen carefully to His words and watch closely His actions. And still some people misunderstood who He is!

OPTION 2: Help-o-matic

Provide each kid with paper and a pencil. Ask kids to draw a picture of a machine that could help them do something they have trouble with or really don't like doing. Allow kids opportunities to share about their machines. What do they do? How would their machines work? How much might they cost?

· paper
· pencils
· markers or crayons

SAY • It can be fun to imagine machines that help us in our everyday lives. Maybe someday you all will even find a way to invent your machines for real! Today we are going to learn about some things Jesus did to help people and heal them. But He did not need special machines or technology because He is God and has power to do miracles.

Transition to teach the story

TEACH the Story

SESSION TITLE: Jesus' Early Miracles
BIBLE PASSAGE: Mark 1
STORY POINT: People came to Jesus, and He healed them.
KEY PASSAGE: John 3:16
BIG PICTURE QUESTION: What makes people special? People are special because we are made in God's image, as male and female, to know Him.

· room decorations
· Theme Background Slide (optional)

Suggested Theme Decorating Ideas: Decorate the room to look like the inside of a hospital. Paint foam board to look like an ambulance parked in a receiving bay. Set medical equipment toys on a table on the stage. Cover a table with a sheet to look like a gurney. You may display the theme background slide.

Countdown

· countdown video

Show the countdown video as you transition to teach the story. Set it to end as the session begins.

Introduce the session (3 minutes)

· leader attire
· first aid kit

[Leader enters wearing navy blue cargo pants and a short-sleeve white button-down. He or she is carrying a first aid kit.]

Tip: If you prefer not to use themed content or characters, adapt or omit this introduction.

LEADER • Hey there! It looks like most of you are in good health, so you must not be here because of an emergency. Oddly enough, things are kinda slow right now, so if you were hoping to see some medical drama, you might be a tad disappointed. On a busy day, you might see all the hard work EMTs—that's Emergency Medical Technicians—like me do to get patients to doctors and nurses, who can provide longer term care. Sometimes it even amazes me. I love being a part of it.

I was just about to go on my break, and I'd love to tell you about an even more amazing situation. EMTs use medical technology to help people, but Jesus used His power as God to help people. I'll tell you about it.

Big picture question (1 minute)

LEADER • As we get to the story, I want to ask a big picture question. While listening to the story, see if you can figure out the answer. *What makes people special?* As we hear our story, you'll see that Jesus cares a lot about people. I want you to think about why that is. I'll make sure we all know the answer after you hear the story.

Giant timeline (1 minute)

Show the giant timeline. Point to individual Bible stories as you review.

·Giant Timeline

LEADER • After sin entered the world, God could have said "too bad, you had your chance." It would have been fair for Him to say that. Instead, God had a plan to defeat sin and death forever. It required a Savior, and after hundreds and hundreds of years, that Savior was born in Bethlehem. Jesus—the fully God and fully human Savior—grew into a man. He was wise and perfectly obeyed God. He was baptized and then resisted temptation to sin in the wilderness. John pointed to Him, and He called disciples to follow Him. Now, Jesus' ministry of teaching and healing was coming into full swing. Today we will learn about "Jesus' Early Miracles."

Tell the Bible story (10 minutes)

- Bibles
- "Jesus' Early Miracles" video
- Big Picture Question Poster
- Bible Story Picture Poster
- Story Point Poster

Open your Bible to Mark 1. Use the Bible storytelling tips on the Bible story page to help you tell the story, or show the Bible story video "Jesus' Early Miracles."

LEADER • People came to Jesus, and He healed them. I want to make sure you noticed two things: first, Jesus consistently had compassion on people who were sick; second, Jesus specifically said that the reason He came was to preach.

Jesus saw the pain and suffering of the people around Him, and He worked to help them. He did not just say, "Oh, that's sad. I'm sorry you are sick." He actually met their physical needs by healing them. Jesus is compassionate and kind. He cares about people and wants to help us.

Even though Jesus' miraculous healings and command over evil spirits were incredible, He wanted His teaching to be the focus of His work. When Jesus wanted to move on, He specifically said that He came to preach. His message of repenting of sin, loving God, and loving people was more important than His power to heal.

It is easy for us to focus only on what God can do for us. We don't always do a good job remembering what God has commanded us to do. Jesus loves us, and He is able to heal and restore, but He also wants us to love and obey God. The most important healing is not physical, but spiritual. Jesus heals us from the damage caused by sin.

What makes people special? People are special because we are made in His image, as male and female, to know Him. Jesus cares about people because He created us. He wants what is best for us, and that is to love and obey God.

Christ connection

LEADER • All of us are born as sinners. The Bible says we are dead in sin. We cannot save ourselves. Thankfully, God's perfect plan was to send His Son, Jesus, to die for our sin and give new life to everyone who believes in Jesus.

Jesus' miracles proved that Jesus is the Messiah, the Son of God. They strengthened people's faith and met their needs. Through Jesus, God did what is impossible for us to do on our own. He provided forgiveness, salvation, and eternal life.

Note: You may use this opportunity to use Scripture and the guide provided to explain how to become a Christian. Make sure kids know when and where they can ask questions.

Questions from kids video (3 minutes)

Show the "Unit 21, Session 1" questions from kids video. Prompt kids to think about who can work miracles. Guide them to discuss ways we see God at work today.

· "Unit 21, Session 1" Questions from Kids video

Missions moment (3 minutes)

Play the "Better Than Basketball" missions video.

LEADER • Every sport you play and every hobby you enjoy can be used to share the love of Jesus. In the Bible, we read that **people came to Jesus, and He healed them**. Jesus heals people today, too, by forgiving their sins and offering eternal life. This week, let's think about all the different ways God can work in our lives to spread the good news about Jesus.

· "Better Than Basketball" missions video

Key passage (5 minutes)

Show the key passage poster. Lead the boys and girls to read

· Key Passage Poster
· "In This Way (John 3:16)" song

Among the People

together John 3:16. Then sing "In This Way (John 3:16)."

LEADER • This key passage might be one of the most well-known verses in the entire Bible. Many people have heard it, memorized it, or seen it as a bumper sticker. In a way, this key passage sums up the whole Bible. God loved us and showed His love by sending Jesus. Everyone who has faith in Jesus won't be punished for sin, but will live forever with God.

Sing (4 minutes)

· "Jesus Messiah" song

LEADER • Jesus healed people who were sick, and He made the way for us to be forgiven of sin and healed of the damage it causes in our lives. He is the Messiah.

Sing together "Jesus Messiah."

Pray (2 minutes)

Invite kids to pray before dismissing to apply the story.

LEADER • Father, thank You for sending Jesus. We can hardly understand Your love. Help us love You back. Give us the courage we need to obey You in difficult circumstances. Fill our hearts with compassion for others. Amen.

Dismiss to apply the story

The Gospel: God's Plan for Me

Ask kids if they have ever heard the word *gospel*. Clarify that the word *gospel* means "good news." It is the message about Christ, the kingdom of God, and salvation. Use the following guide to share the gospel with kids.

God rules. Explain to kids that the Bible tells us God created everything, and He is in charge of everything. Invite a volunteer to read Genesis 1:1 from the Bible. Read Revelation 4:11 or Colossians 1:16-17 aloud and explain what these verses mean.

We sinned. Tell kids that since the time of Adam and Eve, everyone has chosen to disobey God. (Romans 3:23) The Bible calls this sin. Because God is holy, God cannot be around sin. Sin separates us from God and deserves God's punishment of death. (Romans 6:23)

God provided. Choose a child to read John 3:16 aloud. Say that God sent His Son, Jesus, the perfect solution to our sin problem, to rescue us from the punishment we deserve. It's something we, as sinners, could never earn on our own. Jesus alone saves us. Read and explain Ephesians 2:8-9.

Jesus gives. Share with kids that Jesus lived a perfect life, died on the cross for our sins, and rose again. Because Jesus gave up His life for us, we can be welcomed into God's family for eternity. This is the best gift ever! Read Romans 5:8; 2 Corinthians 5:21; or 1 Peter 3:18.

We respond. Tell kids that they can respond to Jesus. Read Romans 10:9-10,13. Review these aspects of our response: Believe in your heart that Jesus alone saves you through what He's already done on the cross. Repent, turning from self and sin to Jesus. Tell God and others that your faith is in Jesus.

Offer to talk with any child who is interested in responding to Jesus. Provide *I'm a Christian Now!* for new Christians to take home and complete with their families.

APPLY the Story

SESSION TITLE: Jesus' Early Miracles
BIBLE PASSAGE: Mark 1
STORY POINT: People came to Jesus, and He healed them.
KEY PASSAGE: John 3:16
BIG PICTURE QUESTION: What makes people special? People are special because we are made in God's image, as male and female, to know Him.

Key passage activity (5 minutes)

· Key Passage Poster
· marker
· large sheet of paper or poster board
· Bibles (optional)

Read the key passage aloud with the kids multiple times. Then hide or cover the key passage poster. Write the key passage incorrectly on a large sheet of paper or poster board, and challenge the kids to help you correct it. You may give out Bibles and challenge the kids to use their Bibles to find the verse.

> Suggested incorrect passage:
> "For *Jesus liked* the world in this way: He *took* His one and only *Father* so that everyone who *wonders* in Him will not *sneeze* but have *eventual* life."

SAY • Great job fixing those mistakes. God's Word is perfect and true, and memorizing it is a wonderful way to make sure we have the truth with us all the time. This key passage, when read correctly, helps us understand the gospel. God loves people and showed His love by sending Jesus to save us from sin.

Discussion & Bible skills (10 minutes)

· Bibles, 1 per kid
· Story Point Poster
· Small Group Timeline and Map Set (005802970, optional)

Distribute a Bible to each kid. Help kids find Mark 1. You may select a strong reader to find and read aloud select verses. Show where the story took place on the New

Testament Israel Map. (*D6*)

Ask the following questions. Lead the group to discuss:

Option: Retell or review the Bible story using the bolded text of the Bible story script.

1. Where was the synagogue in which Jesus taught? (*Capernaum, Mark 1:21*)

2. Why did Jesus say He came? (*to teach, Mark 1:38*)

3. Why did Jesus heal the man with leprosy? (*Jesus had compassion on him, Mark 1:41*)

4. What do these miracles show about Jesus? *Guide kids to discuss Jesus' power as God's Son. Jesus had authority over evil spirits and over the sickness people faced. We also see Jesus' love and kindness toward people. Jesus meets physical needs and spiritual needs.*

5. Why was Jesus' preaching more important than His miracles? *Help kids understand that Jesus' miracles helped to show His power and authority, but the purpose was to support the truth of His teaching. A person healed of a sickness might later become sick again and is still spiritually dead in sin. A person who understands Jesus' teaching and has faith in His death and resurrection is forgiven and gains eternal life.*

6. How can we be like Jesus? *Discuss Jesus' compassion, kindness, and preaching. Help kids see that we can show God's love in the way we treat others. Explain that our love and kindness will help support the message of truth when we share the gospel. Actions may "speak louder" than words, but words are still essential for explaining the gospel.*

SAY • **People came to Jesus, and He healed them**. Jesus loves people. His greatest miracle happened when Jesus died and rose again to destroy sin's power. Everyone who trusts in Jesus is saved from sin and can be healed of the damage sin causes.

Activity choice (10 minutes)

OPTION 1: On mission

Print the "On Missions Statements" printable and cut apart each statement. Tape the statements to a basketball. Then invite kids to sit in a circle and roll the basketball to one another. When you say stop, the person with the ball will complete the statement facing him. If you prefer, let the player choose the statement he wants to answer. Continue play as time allows.

SAY • Each of us can be part of God's mission to reach the world with the message of Jesus. Some missionaries, like Heiden Ratner in Nevada, use basketball or other sports to bring people to Jesus. God wants to use us—no matter our gifts or skills—to share the good news with the world.

OPTION 2: Prayer time

Open your Bible to Mark 1:35.

SAY • **People came to Jesus, and He healed them**. Jesus has power because He is the Son of God. Even though Jesus has incredible power to work miracles, He still needed time to pray to God. If Jesus chose to spend time praying, it must be extremely important for us to spend time praying too. Prayer is talking to God. We can talk to God just as we would talk to a friend or our parents. We can pray about anything.

Lead the kids in a time of guided prayer. Remind them that they do not have to pray aloud if they feel uncomfortable doing so. Encourage them to pray about more than just things they want, but also to pray as a way to praise God and thank Him.

- "On Mission Statements" printable
- scissors
- tape
- basketball

Tip: Use this activity option to reinforce the missions moment found in Teach the Story.

LOW PREP

- Bible

Reflection and prayer (5 minutes)

Distribute a sheet of paper to each child. Ask the kids to write about or draw a picture to answer the following questions:

- What does this story teach me about God or about the gospel?
- What does this story teach me about myself?
- Whom can I tell about this story?

Make sure to send the sheets home with kids alongside the activity page so that parents can see what their kids have been learning.

If time remains, take prayer requests or allow kids to complete the Bible story coloring page provided with this session. Pray for your group.

· pencils and crayons
· paper
· Bible Story Coloring Page, 1 per kid

Tip: Give parents this week's *Big Picture Cards for Families* to allow families to interact with the biblical content at home.

Use Week of:

Unit 21 · Session 2
Jesus Taught in Nazareth

BIBLE PASSAGE:
Luke 4

STORY POINT:
Jesus taught that He is the Messiah.

KEY PASSAGE:
John 3:16

BIG PICTURE QUESTION:
What makes people special?
People are special because we are
made in God's image, as male
and female, to know Him.

INTRODUCE THE STORY (10–15 MINUTES) **PAGE 182**		**TEACH THE STORY** (25–30 MINUTES) **PAGE 184**		**APPLY THE STORY** (25–30 MINUTES) **PAGE 190**
	→		→	

Additional resources are available at gospelproject.com. For free training and
session-by-session help, visit MinistryGrid.com/thegospelproject.

LEADER Bible Study

Jesus was about thirty years old when He began His earthly ministry. After John baptized Jesus in the Jordan River, Jesus was tempted in the desert. Jesus traveled to Jerusalem for the Passover. Then He headed north to Galilee. He went through the region of Samaria, stopping at Jacob's well to talk to a Samaritan woman.

After, Jesus went to the town of Nazareth, where He had grown up. Nazareth was a small village in the hills between the Sea of Galilee and the Mediterranean Sea. On the Sabbath day, Jesus went into the synagogue to teach. He read aloud the words of the prophet Isaiah. (See Isa. 61:1-2.) Jesus sat down. Everyone's eyes were on Him as He explained, "Today as you listen, this Scripture has been fulfilled." Jesus was saying, *It's Me*. The words Jesus read were coming true. Some people remembered Jesus from His youth. They asked, "Isn't this Joseph's son?"

Jesus knew their thoughts; Jesus had performed miracles in Capernaum, and the people wanted Jesus to do miracles in His hometown too. Jesus reminded them of two Old Testament accounts. Many widows lived in Israel when the prophet Elijah was there, but God sent Elijah to help a widow in another country. And Elisha likely encountered Israelites who had leprosy, but he healed Naaman the Syrian.

Jesus wanted the people to understand that His miracles were an act of grace—a gift. No one deserves God's grace, so God may show grace to whomever He pleases—even Gentiles. The people were angry about that last part. They drove Jesus away, intending to kill Him, but Jesus escaped through the crowd.

As you teach, explain that Jesus came to give sight to the blind and to set the captives free. He came preaching good news to all the people groups. Finally, the Messiah had come! Jesus was God's plan to save sinners.

Jesus Taught in Nazareth

Luke 4

Jesus went to the town of Nazareth where He had lived when He was a boy. Now Jesus was grown. He traveled all around, teaching people about God. **On the Sabbath day, Jesus went to the synagogue in Nazareth.** The synagogue was a special building where Jews met together to pray, worship, and learn about the Scriptures.

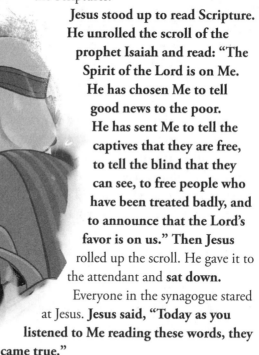

Jesus stood up to read Scripture. He unrolled the scroll of the prophet Isaiah and read: "The Spirit of the Lord is on Me. He has chosen Me to tell good news to the poor. He has sent Me to tell the captives that they are free, to tell the blind that they can see, to free people who have been treated badly, and to announce that the Lord's favor is on us." Then Jesus rolled up the scroll. He gave it to the attendant and **sat down.**

Everyone in the synagogue stared at Jesus. **Jesus said, "Today as you listened to Me reading these words, they came true."**

The people said good things about Jesus, and they were amazed at Him. But some of the people in Nazareth had known Jesus from His youth. "Isn't this Joseph's son?" they asked. Jesus said, "No prophet is accepted in his hometown." Jesus told the people about times when God used prophets to help people who were not Jews. He reminded them of Elijah and Elisha. When there was a terrible famine in Israel and no rain fell there for three and a half years, plenty of widows in the country needed help. But the prophet Elijah did not help the widows in Israel. Instead, God sent Elijah to help a widow in another land.

And when Elisha was a prophet, many people in Israel had leprosy. They wanted to be healed, but Elisha did not heal them. Instead, he healed a man named Naaman (NAY muhn), and Naaman was from Syria—a country that hated God's people.

The people in the synagogue were angry. They forced Jesus out of town. They wanted to throw Him off a cliff, but Jesus walked right through the crowd and went on His way.

Christ Connection: Hundreds of years before Jesus was born, the prophet Isaiah wrote about God's plan to send a Messiah. The Messiah would bring good news and redeem people who were broken and hurting. Jesus read Isaiah's words and announced that He is the promised Messiah.

Bible Storytelling Tips

• **Stand and sit:** Begin the story seated. Stand when Jesus stands and sit back down when He sits.
• **Vary tone:** Speak boldly when speaking Jesus' words. Whisper the questions of the crowd.

INTRODUCE the Story

SESSION TITLE: Jesus Taught in Nazareth
BIBLE PASSAGE: Luke 4
STORY POINT: Jesus taught that He is the Messiah.
KEY PASSAGE: John 3:16
BIG PICTURE QUESTION: What makes people special? People are special because we are made in God's image, as male and female, to know Him.

Welcome time

Greet each kid as he or she arrives. Use this time to collect the offering, fill out attendance sheets, and help new kids connect to your group. Prompt kids to discuss a time they felt accepted, welcomed, or loved.

SAY • We all enjoy feeling accepted and loved. Jesus accepts us as we are and loves us despite our sin. Today, we will learn about a time Jesus was not accepted, but rejected! People did not believe the truth about Him and used force to make Him leave.

Activity page (5 minutes)

· "Rejected" activity page, 1 per kid
· pencils or markers

Invite kids to complete the "Rejected" activity page. Encourage kids to scan the Bible story picture and circle all the silly items that do not belong in the picture.

SAY • Good job finding the things that don't belong. You rejected those items from the picture because they should not have been there. Today we will hear about a time people rejected Jesus. Why do you think people might reject Jesus?

Session starter (10 minutes)

OPTION 1: Accept or reject

LOW PREP

Direct kids to sit in a circle. Select a kid to go first. She will turn to the kid on her left and make a silly offer. He must say "accepted" or "rejected" based on how he feels about her offer. Then he will make a silly offer to the kid on his left. Play passes in this way until each kid has made an offer.

Suggested offers:
- I'll let you high-five my cactus.
- I'll shave your pet.
- I'll tie your shoes together.
- I'll let you wear my sunglasses at night.

SAY • Those were some silly offers. I don't blame you for rejecting most of them. Today we will learn about a time Jesus was rejected, even though His offer was wonderful and true. Who do you think rejected Jesus?

OPTION 2: Sort it out

· buttons, coins, or plastic gems

Provide each kid with a small handful of buttons. Ask kids to sort the buttons by color, size, and shape. Then instruct the kids to count their buttons and reject all the buttons that have a given trait, such as those that are red, have two holes, or are not round. You may instead use coins, plastic gems, or other small objects.

SAY • You may have a good reason to remove certain objects. For example, if you are replacing a button, you might reject buttons that are the wrong size or color. Today we will learn about a time people rejected Jesus because of what He taught.

Transition to teach the story

TEACH the Story

SESSION TITLE: Jesus Taught in Nazareth
BIBLE PASSAGE: Luke 4
STORY POINT: Jesus taught that He is the Messiah.
KEY PASSAGE: John 3:16
BIG PICTURE QUESTION: What makes people special? People are special because we are made in God's image, as male and female, to know Him.

Countdown

· countdown video

Show the countdown video as you transition to teach the story. Set it to end as the session begins.

Introduce the session (3 minutes)

· leader attire
· first aid kit

[Leader enters wearing navy blue cargo pants and a short-sleeve white button-down. He or she is carrying a first aid kit.]

Tip: If you prefer not to use themed content or characters, adapt or omit this introduction.

LEADER • Hey, everyone! It's very nice to see you again. To those of you who are new, I'm glad to meet you. I'm an Emergency Medical Technician—an EMT—so I spend a lot of time either in an ambulance or in a hospital. I really enjoy my job because it's a great way to help people. If someone calls for an ambulance, I might show up on the scene to provide medical care until we reach a hospital, where doctors and nurses can take over.

That is, of course, assuming you agree to come with me in the ambulance. If someone calls an ambulance for you, you can choose whether or not you want to go with the EMTs. I recently met a man who had just been in a car collision. Another driver on the road called 911, and I happened to be working that shift. When I arrived, the driver in the accident was up, walking around, and had called a friend to come pick him up. We offered to take him to the hospital to get checked out just in case, but he said he didn't want to. Thankfully, he was not hurt.

In a way, that reminds me of a Bible story. Jesus was explaining to some people who He is and how He can help them, but they rejected Him and His help. I'll tell you all about it.

Big picture question (1 minute)

LEADER • We know that Jesus helped many people. That leads us to our big picture question: *What makes people special? People are special because we are made in God's image, as male and female, to know Him.* God created us and loves us. He sent Jesus to save us because we are special to Him. Nothing else God created is described as made in God's image. Human beings—men, women, and children—are unique in that way. It sets us apart from all other created things.

Giant timeline (1 minute)

Show the giant timeline. Point to individual Bible stories as you review.

·Giant Timeline

LEADER • After Jesus was baptized and tempted in the wilderness, He called disciples and began His public ministry. We learned last week that Jesus traveled around teaching amazing things about God. **People came to Jesus, and He healed them**. This week, we will learn what happened when Jesus went back to where He grew up to teach people about Himself.

Our story is called "Jesus Taught in Nazareth."

Tell the Bible story (10 minutes)

· Bibles
· "Jesus Taught in
  Nazareth" video
· Big Picture Question
  Poster
· Bible Story Picture
  Poster
· Story Point Poster

Open your Bible to Luke 4. Use the Bible storytelling tips on the Bible story page to help you tell the story, or show the Bible story video "Jesus Taught in Nazareth."

LEADER • One of my favorite things about the Bible is how it all fits together to tell one story. Jesus proved this when He read from the scroll of Isaiah. The prophecy talked about captives being set free. It said that there would be someone anointed by God to bring good news. Jesus explained that He is the One Isaiah had written about 700 years earlier.

Jesus taught that He is the Messiah. At first, the people seemed pretty impressed—and maybe a little confused. But when Jesus reminded them of how Elijah and Elisha helped people from outside Israel, the people in the synagogue became angry. To understand why, we need to understand what Jesus was teaching them.

God's plan all along was to use the nation of Israel. God promised to bless them to bless the world. Over time, many of the Jewish people began to see God's blessings as something only for them, not for other nations. Jesus was reminding them that God's love doesn't stop with Jewish people, but extends out to all people. All people are special to God. *What makes people special? People are special because we are made in God's image, as male and female, to know Him*.

Jesus was teaching them that His role in God's plan was not to make Israel powerful again, but to bring salvation to all nations—to everyone who believes in Him. This was God's plan all along.

Christ connection

LEADER • Hundreds of years before Jesus was born, the prophet Isaiah wrote about God's plan to send a Messiah. The Messiah would bring good news and redeem people who were broken and hurting. Jesus read Isaiah's words and announced that He is the promised Messiah.

Many of the religious leaders rejected Jesus because they did not want to believe that their sin was very bad. Even today some people reject Jesus because they believe they do not need a Savior. They may not believe that Jesus is who He said He is. But that should not stop us from teaching the truth.

Note: You may use this opportunity to use Scripture and the guide provided to explain how to become a Christian. Make sure kids know when and where they can ask questions.

Questions from kids video (3 minutes)

Show the "Unit 21, Session 2" questions from kids video. Prompt kids to think about who rejects Jesus. Guide them to discuss what they love about Jesus or any questions they have about following Him.

· "Unit 21, Session 2" Questions from Kids video

🌐 Missions moment (3 minutes)

Display the "Las Vegas Photos" printable in the room or prepare to pass copies of it around for kids to see. As they examine the pictures, ask them to comment on some of the sites they see.

· "Las Vegas Photos" printable

LEADER • Las Vegas, Nevada, is a busy city and a popular spot for tourists. It's also a city where many people ignore Jesus and live without hope. **Jesus taught that He is the Messiah**, but many people still don't have faith in Him. Some Christians have chosen to live in Las Vegas to teach people the truth about the gospel and the hope that Jesus gives. God wants the people in this popular city to turn away from sin and turn to Him.

Key passage (5 minutes)

· Key Passage Poster
· "In This Way (John 3:16)" song

Show the key passage poster. Lead the boys and girls to read together John 3:16. Then sing "In This Way (John 3:16)."

LEADER • Our key passage reminds us of the gospel. God showed His love for people by sending Jesus. Jesus is God's Son, and everyone who believes in Him will live forever with God.

Sing (4 minutes)

· "Take It to the Lord" song

LEADER • Jesus loves even those who reject Him. We must call on Him to be saved, but He loves even those who refuse to accept the gift of salvation. He is the best friend we could ever have.

Sing together "Take It to the Lord."

Pray (2 minutes)

Invite kids to pray before dismissing to apply the story.

LEADER • Thank You, Lord, for sending Jesus to be the Messiah. Thank You for loving us even in our sin. We know that we need You. Help us obey You out of love. Give us courage to tell others about You and protect us from feeling discouraged when others reject Jesus. Amen.

Dismiss to apply the story

The Gospel: God's Plan for Me

Ask kids if they have ever heard the word *gospel*. Clarify that the word *gospel* means "good news." It is the message about Christ, the kingdom of God, and salvation. Use the following guide to share the gospel with kids.

God rules. Explain to kids that the Bible tells us God created everything, and He is in charge of everything. Invite a volunteer to read Genesis 1:1 from the Bible. Read Revelation 4:11 or Colossians 1:16-17 aloud and explain what these verses mean.

We sinned. Tell kids that since the time of Adam and Eve, everyone has chosen to disobey God. (Romans 3:23) The Bible calls this sin. Because God is holy, God cannot be around sin. Sin separates us from God and deserves God's punishment of death. (Romans 6:23)

God provided. Choose a child to read John 3:16 aloud. Say that God sent His Son, Jesus, the perfect solution to our sin problem, to rescue us from the punishment we deserve. It's something we, as sinners, could never earn on our own. Jesus alone saves us. Read and explain Ephesians 2:8-9.

Jesus gives. Share with kids that Jesus lived a perfect life, died on the cross for our sins, and rose again. Because Jesus gave up His life for us, we can be welcomed into God's family for eternity. This is the best gift ever! Read Romans 5:8; 2 Corinthians 5:21; or 1 Peter 3:18.

We respond. Tell kids that they can respond to Jesus. Read Romans 10:9-10,13. Review these aspects of our response: Believe in your heart that Jesus alone saves you through what He's already done on the cross. Repent, turning from self and sin to Jesus. Tell God and others that your faith is in Jesus.

Offer to talk with any child who is interested in responding to Jesus. Provide *I'm a Christian Now!* for new Christians to take home and complete with their families.

APPLY the Story

SESSION TITLE: Jesus Taught in Nazareth
BIBLE PASSAGE: Luke 4
STORY POINT: Jesus taught that He is the Messiah.
KEY PASSAGE: John 3:16
BIG PICTURE QUESTION: What makes people special? People are special because we are made in God's image, as male and female, to know Him.

Key passage activity (5 minutes)

- Key Passage Poster
- "Key Passage Flip Cards" Printable
- pencils

Print the "Key Passage Flip Cards" printable double sided onto heavyweight paper using the translation of your choice. Then cut them apart. Help the kids fold the cards in half so that only one level is visible at a time. The kids will start on level one and fill in the missing words. After completing each level, kids will flip the card and fold back the completed levels to work on the next level without peeking at the completed levels.

SAY • This key passage, recorded by John, is words spoken by Jesus Himself. Jesus explained that God showed His love by sending a Rescuer to save people from sin. We can have eternal life with God by believing in Jesus' death and resurrection for our sin. That is the good news of the gospel. God loves us in this way because all people are special to Him.

Discussion & Bible skills (10 minutes)

- Bibles, 1 per kid
- Story Point Poster
- Small Group Timeline and Map Set (005802970, optional)

Distribute a Bible to each kid. Help kids find Luke 4. You may use the New Testament Israel Map to show the kids where Nazareth is located. (E5) Remind kids that Luke is part of the Gospels, along with Matthew, Mark, and John.

Ask the following questions. Lead the group to discuss:

Option: Retell or review the Bible story using the bolded text of the Bible story script.

1. Where did Jesus grow up? (*Nazareth, Luke 4:16*)
2. From whose scroll did Jesus read? (*the prophet Isaiah's, Luke 4:17*)
3. How did the people react to Jesus? (*amazed and confused at first, then angry; Luke 4:22,28*)
4. How do we know Jesus really is the Messiah? *Guide kids to discuss the overwhelming evidence that Jesus is the Messiah. Remind them of all the prophecies that Jesus fulfilled, such as His birth in Bethlehem. Point out His power to heal people and remind them that God called Jesus His Son. Jesus' claim in this story is well supported by other evidence.*
5. What does it mean to accept Jesus rather than reject Him? *Help kids see that when our faith is in Jesus, we are doing more than admitting that He is the Messiah, we are also saying that He is the Lord of our lives. When we believe in Jesus, we are saying that we want Him to guide and control our lives. We want to obey Him out of love and serve Him to glorify God.*
6. What can we do if we know someone who rejects Jesus? *Remind kids that we cannot save anyone. Our job when we believe the gospel is to teach other people about Jesus. Help kids understand that God is the One who saves people. Discuss the importance of prayer in leading others to Jesus. Make sure they know that we treat everyone with kindness and respect, even if they don't yet believe the gospel.*

SAY • **Jesus taught that He is the Messiah**. Jesus loves people and wants to see everyone rescued from sin. We cannot make people believe, but we can tell them the good news so they can believe and be saved.

Activity choice (10 minutes)

- brightly colored heavyweight paper
- brightly colored chenille stems
- glue
- scissors
- markers

Tip: Use this activity option to reinforce the missions moment found in Teach the Story.

OPTION 1: Bright signs

Provide each kid with a brightly colored sheet of heavyweight paper. Help the kids use brightly colored chenille stems to form the letters *J*, *E*, *S*, *U*, and *S*. Kids will then glue the chenille stem letters to their heavyweight paper. Allow time for kids to cut their signs into interesting shapes. You may provide markers for kids to write additional words to add to the sign messages.

SAY • Las Vegas is full of neon signs that mark popular tourist spots, restaurants, and hotels. Missionaries go into this busy city with all the neon lights to tell people about Jesus and start churches. Hang your sign somewhere you will see daily to remind you to shine brightly for Jesus.

LOW PREP

- masking tape

OPTION 2: Along the line

Use tape to mark a line down the center of the room. Designate one end as "good" and the other as "not good." Ask the kids to stand somewhere along the line based on how they feel about themselves in regards to different criteria, such as their skill at dancing, their ability to draw, or their feelings about eating vegetables. End by asking them how they feel about their spiritual life. Ask them where along the line a person would be to need Jesus to rescue him or her.

SAY • We sometimes make the mistake of thinking certain sinful choices are worse than others. Some people may think they are good enough and don't need a Rescuer. Some people may think they are so bad that they cannot be rescued. The truth is, everyone who is on the line needs rescuing. There's no such thing as being "too good to need Jesus" or "too bad for Jesus to save you." We all need to be rescued.

Jesus taught that He is the Messiah. He alone can save us when we ask Him to. And He wants to see all people saved!

Reflection and prayer (5 minutes)

Distribute a sheet of paper to each child. Ask the kids to write about or draw a picture to answer the following questions:

- What does this story teach me about God or about the gospel?
- What does this story teach me about myself?
- Whom can I tell about this story?

Make sure to send the sheets home with kids alongside the activity page so that parents can see what their kids have been learning.

If time remains, take prayer requests or allow kids to complete the Bible story coloring page provided with this session. Pray for your group.

· pencils and crayons
· paper
· Bible Story Coloring Page, 1 per kid

Tip: Give parents this week's *Big Picture Cards for Families* to allow families to interact with the biblical content at home.

Use Week of:

Unit 21 · Session 3
Jesus and Nicodemus

BIBLE PASSAGE:
John 3

STORY POINT:
Jesus taught that we must
be born again.

KEY PASSAGE:
John 3:16

BIG PICTURE QUESTION:
What makes people special?
People are special because we are
made in God's image, as male
and female, to know Him.

INTRODUCE THE STORY	TEACH THE STORY	APPLY THE STORY
(10–15 MINUTES)	(25–30 MINUTES)	(25–30 MINUTES)
PAGE 198	**PAGE 200**	**PAGE 206**

 → →

Additional resources are available at gospelproject.com. For free training and
session-by-session help, visit MinistryGrid.com/thegospelproject.

LEADER Bible Study

Jesus' ministry had begun. His early miracles included turning water into wine, casting out demons, and healing people. John 2:23 says that "many believed in his name when they saw the signs he was doing." Jesus likely spent a large part of His day teaching. When the day was done, He spent time alone or with His disciples. One night, a man named Nicodemus approached Jesus.

Nicodemus was a Pharisee and a ruler of the Jews; that is, he was a religious leader who taught God's law, and he was a member of the Sanhedrin—a Jewish governing body. Nicodemus held to the belief that if a person was a law-abiding Jew, he would be accepted by God. Jesus gave Nicodemus a lesson that would turn his belief system on its head.

Jesus was a carpenter (Mark 6:3), so the religious teachers likely assumed He didn't know theology. But they had seen Jesus' miraculous signs in Jerusalem. Nicodemus had to conclude, "You are a teacher who has come from God" (John 3:2).

Nicodemus initiated the conversation, but Jesus chose the subject. His words perplexed Nicodemus: "Unless someone is born again, he cannot see the kingdom of God" (John 3:3). Jesus explained that spiritual birth is not unlike physical birth in that a person cannot do it himself; it is something that happens to him.

Jesus reminded Nicodemus of an Old Testament account, the disobedient Israelites and the bronze snake. The Israelites could not help themselves, but when they trusted in God and looked to the bronze snake lifted up on the pole, they were healed. (Num. 21:4-9)

Emphasize to kids that every person is born a sinner—spiritually dead and alienated from God. It is by God's Spirit—not our own effort—that we are born again. We look to Jesus and His finished work on the cross for our salvation.

Among the People

The **BIBLE** Story

Jesus and Nicodemus

John 3

Jesus was in Jerusalem for the Passover feast. **One night, a religious man came to see Jesus. The man's name was Nicodemus.** Nicodemus was a Pharisee. He studied and taught God's law, and he tried very hard to   obey the law. **Nicodemus wanted to know more about Jesus.**

"Rabbi," he said, "we know that You are a teacher who has come from God. No one could do the miracles You do unless God were with him."

Nicodemus had that right. **Jesus said, "I tell you: Unless someone is born again, he cannot see the kingdom of God."**

Now Nicodemus was confused. He thought that keeping all God's laws was how a person got into heaven. Besides, what Jesus said didn't make any sense! **"How can anyone be born when he is old?" Nicodemus asked.**

Jesus said, "A person cannot enter God's kingdom unless he is born of water and the Spirit. Whatever is born of the flesh is flesh, and whatever is born of the Spirit is spirit." **When a baby is born, he gets physical life from his parents. Physical life doesn't last forever. But the Spirit gives people a better kind of life—spiritual life—so**

Younger Kids Leader Guide
Unit 21 • Session 3

they can live with God forever.

Jesus said, "Don't be surprised I told you that you must be born again."

Nicodemus still didn't understand. "How is this possible?" he asked.

Jesus said, "When you don't believe what I say about things I've seen on earth, how will you believe what I say about the things I've seen in heaven? **Do you remember how Moses raised up the bronze snake in the wilderness? Everyone who looked at it was healed. Like that, the Son of Man will be raised up, so that everyone who believes in Him will have eternal life.**"

Then Jesus told Nicodemus about God's great plan. Jesus said, "**God loved the world in this way: He gave His one and only Son, so that everyone who believes in Him will not perish but have eternal life.** God did not send His Son to declare the world guilty, but to save the world. Anyone who believes in Him is found not guilty, but anyone who does not believe in Him is guilty already."

Christ Connection: Nicodemus needed new life—eternal life—but he could not do anything to earn it. Eternal life is a gift that comes only from God. God showed His love in this way: He sent His one and only Son to save the world. Everyone who believes in Him will not perish but will have eternal life.

Bible Storytelling Tips

- **Call for active listening:** Challenge kids to count how many times they hear the word *born* in the story.
- **Vary your voice:** Vary your voice for the dialogue of different people. For example, use one voice for Jesus and another voice for Nicodemus.

INTRODUCE the Story

SESSION TITLE: Jesus and Nicodemus

BIBLE PASSAGE: John 3

STORY POINT: Jesus taught that we must be born again.

KEY PASSAGE: John 3:16

BIG PICTURE QUESTION: What makes people special? People are special because we are made in God's image, as male and female, to know Him.

Welcome time

Greet each kid as he or she arrives. Use this time to collect the offering, fill out attendance sheets, and help new kids connect to your group. Prompt kids to tell about times they needed extra help to understand something.

SAY • All of us need help understanding new things. That's what makes teachers so great! Today, we will learn about a time a man went to Jesus to learn more about Jesus—and the man who went to Jesus was a religious leader who usually taught others!

Activity page (5 minutes)

· "Gospel Plan" activity page, 1 per kid
· pencils or markers

Invite kids to complete the "Gospel Plan" activity page. Encourage kids to draw each symbol from The Gospel: God's Plan For Me. Encourage the kids to practice sharing the gospel with one another, using their activity sheets as guides.

SAY • The gospel is the good news of God's plan to save us. If you memorize these five points, you will be all set to know the gospel and share it with others. Who do you know who needs to hear the gospel?

Session starter (10 minutes)

OPTION 1: I seek

Select a kid to secretly pick an object in the room. She will start the game by telling the other kids the color of the object she is seeking. Other kids must try to figure out what she is seeking and bring it to her if it is possible. Once a kid realizes what she is seeking, allow that kid a chance to pick an object.

SAY • Great job with that game. You sought some great objects. Today we will learn about a man named Nicodemus. He was a religious leader in Jesus' time. He was seeking Jesus. Why do you think Nicodemus sought Jesus?

OPTION 2: The only path

Use tape to mark the floor with a grid pattern. On a sheet of paper, draw the same grid pattern and color in certain squares on the grid to designate the "only path" from one side of the grid to the other. Keep the piece of paper with the "only path" markings hidden from all the kids. Allow kids to take turns trying to cross the taped grid on the floor. Stop each kid as he or she steps on unsafe squares. You may wish to have backup "only path" keys prepared in case your group has time to play again.

· tape
· paper
· pen

SAY • Great job finding the only path. In our story today, we will learn about a man who wished to know how to be saved. He met with Jesus at night to learn about the only way to be with God forever. What do you think Jesus taught him?

Transition to teach the story

Among the People

TEACH the Story

SESSION TITLE: Jesus and Nicodemus
BIBLE PASSAGE: John 3
STORY POINT: Jesus taught that we must be born again.
KEY PASSAGE: John 3:16
BIG PICTURE QUESTION: What makes people special? People are special because we are made in God's image, as male and female, to know Him.

Countdown

· countdown video

Show the countdown video as you transition to teach the story. Set it to end as the session begins.

Introduce the session (3 minutes)

· leader attire
· first aid kit

[Leader enters wearing navy blue cargo pants and a short-sleeve white button-down. He or she is carrying a first aid kit.]

LEADER • My goodness! I am very tired. One of the harder parts of being an Emergency Medical Technician is the late-night shift. As you can imagine, emergencies might happen at any time, so there are always some EMTs working late to be ready. It just so happened that my night working late was last night.

Tip: If you prefer not to use themed content or characters, adapt or omit this introduction.

Thankfully, it was a slow night. We had only one emergency call, and the patient is going to make a full recovery. Apparently he wanted to do some yard work at night because the sun makes it too hot for him. It was a dangerous choice, and now he knows better than to use a hedge trimmer in the dark.

But you know, as silly as it might sound, the nighttime emergency makes me think of a Bible story. A man named Nicodemus visited Jesus in the nighttime. He wasn't having a medical emergency, but he and Jesus did talk about being saved. Here, I'll tell you all about it.

Big picture question (1 minute)

LEADER • Remember, we have been learning about Jesus' interactions with people. Our big picture question is ***What makes people special? People are special because we are made in God's image, as male and female, to know Him***. God did not create us because He needed us, but because He wanted to share His goodness with people by having a personal relationship with us. Sin breaks our relationship with God, but we are special to God. He loves us even though we are born in sin. God's love is a huge part of why He sent Jesus to save us.

Giant timeline (1 minute)

Show the giant timeline. Point to individual Bible stories as you review.

· Giant Timeline

LEADER • A few weeks back, we learned about Jesus' early miracles. **People came to Jesus, and He healed them**. Then we learned that while in Nazareth, **Jesus taught that He is the Messiah**. Many of the people seemed open to that, until Jesus reminded them that God's plan was for Gentiles as well as Jews. They rejected Jesus and rushed Him out of the synagogue. This week, we will learn about a religious leader named Nicodemus, who wanted to learn more about Jesus and met Him in secret. Our story is called "Jesus and Nicodemus."

Tell the Bible story (10 minutes)

· Bibles
· "Jesus and Nicodemus" video
· Big Picture Question Poster
· Bible Story Picture Poster
· Story Point Poster

Open your Bible to John 3. Use the Bible storytelling tips on the Bible story page to help you tell the story, or show the Bible story video "Jesus and Nicodemus."

LEADER • Many of the religious leaders in Jesus' time rejected Jesus, like in the story we learned last week. Nicodemus was wise to try to learn more about Jesus. But what Jesus said confused him. **Jesus taught that we must be born again**.

Nicodemus struggled to understand the difference between physical life and spiritual life. We often struggle in the same way. We can see, smell, taste, touch, and hear the different parts of our physical lives. It is easy to think that the world we can observe with our senses is all there is, but Jesus explained that there's more than what we can interact with. We need to be born spiritually into Jesus' family.

The reason Jesus describes salvation in this way has to do with what happens to us when we put our faith in Jesus. Our old, sinful lives die, and we receive new hearts from God. Our new hearts love God and want to obey Him. It is as if we become entirely new people. The Bible says the old is gone and the new has come. That new life cannot be taken away.

Christ connection

Note: You may use this opportunity to use Scripture and the guide provided to explain how to become a Christian. Make sure kids know when and where they can ask questions.

LEADER • Nicodemus needed new life—eternal life—but he could not do anything to earn it. Eternal life is a gift that comes only from God. God showed His love in this way: He sent His one and only Son to save the world. Everyone who believes in Him will not perish but will have eternal life.

Questions from kids video (3 minutes)

Show the "Unit 21, Session 3" questions from kids video. Prompt kids to think about how it feels to trust in Jesus. Guide them to discuss how something can be true regardless of our feelings.

· "Unit 21, Session 3" Questions from Kids video

Missions moment (3 minutes)

Play the "Anna's Story" missions video. Then pray that more people in Nevada will know Jesus and choose to follow Him.

· "Anna's Story" missions video

LEADER • **Jesus taught that we must be born again.** As Christians, we want other people to know this, too. We can all have eternal life in heaven through Jesus. In Nevada, a young woman named Anna asked, "What can I do to have a relationship with Christ?" Missionaries Heiden and Neena Ratner and Christian athletes of Walk Church introduced Anna to Jesus and taught her how to be born again. If someone asked you how to have a relationship with Jesus, what would you say?

Key passage (5 minutes)

Show the key passage poster. Lead the boys and girls to read together John 3:16. Then sing "In This Way (John 3:16)."

· Key Passage Poster
· "In This Way (John 3:16)" song

LEADER • This key passage tells us something wonderful about God. God doesn't just love people, He loves us in a specific way: He sent Jesus to die on the cross for our sin. Jesus explained this to Nicodemus in our story today. Everyone who trusts Jesus will have life with God that lasts forever.

Sing (4 minutes)

· "Jesus Messiah" song

LEADER • Let's sing praises to Jesus, the chosen One sent by God to save us. He is the Messiah.

Sing together "Jesus Messiah."

Pray (2 minutes)

Invite kids to pray before dismissing to apply the story.

LEADER • Lord, thank You for showing Your incredible love for us through Jesus. Help us love You and obey Your commands. Give us ears that can hear You and hearts that can feel You. We want to know You and be born again into Your family. Amen.

Dismiss to apply the story

The Gospel: God's Plan for Me

Ask kids if they have ever heard the word *gospel*. Clarify that the word *gospel* means "good news." It is the message about Christ, the kingdom of God, and salvation. Use the following guide to share the gospel with kids.

God rules. Explain to kids that the Bible tells us God created everything, and He is in charge of everything. Invite a volunteer to read Genesis 1:1 from the Bible. Read Revelation 4:11 or Colossians 1:16-17 aloud and explain what these verses mean.

We sinned. Tell kids that since the time of Adam and Eve, everyone has chosen to disobey God. (Romans 3:23) The Bible calls this sin. Because God is holy, God cannot be around sin. Sin separates us from God and deserves God's punishment of death. (Romans 6:23)

God provided. Choose a child to read John 3:16 aloud. Say that God sent His Son, Jesus, the perfect solution to our sin problem, to rescue us from the punishment we deserve. It's something we, as sinners, could never earn on our own. Jesus alone saves us. Read and explain Ephesians 2:8-9.

Jesus gives. Share with kids that Jesus lived a perfect life, died on the cross for our sins, and rose again. Because Jesus gave up His life for us, we can be welcomed into God's family for eternity. This is the best gift ever! Read Romans 5:8; 2 Corinthians 5:21; or 1 Peter 3:18.

We respond. Tell kids that they can respond to Jesus. Read Romans 10:9-10,13. Review these aspects of our response: Believe in your heart that Jesus alone saves you through what He's already done on the cross. Repent, turning from self and sin to Jesus. Tell God and others that your faith is in Jesus.

Offer to talk with any child who is interested in responding to Jesus. Provide *I'm a Christian Now!* for new Christians to take home and complete with their families.

APPLY the Story

SESSION TITLE: Jesus and Nicodemus

BIBLE PASSAGE: John 3

STORY POINT: Jesus taught that we must be born again.

KEY PASSAGE: John 3:16

BIG PICTURE QUESTION: What makes people special? People are special because we are made in God's image, as male and female, to know Him.

Key passage activity (5 minutes)

- Key Passage Poster
- marker
- craft sticks

Write each word or phrase of the key passage on a separate craft stick. You may wish to make more than one set. Allow the kids to scatter the sticks and take turns grabbing the sticks to arrange the passage in order. After playing a few rounds, invite volunteers to say the passage from memory. Thank each kid for her effort and encourage all the kids to continue working to memorize John 3:16.

SAY • This key passage was spoken by Jesus to Nicodemus. Jesus summarized the core of the gospel in these few phrases. God loves people. He showed His great love by sending Jesus to be the Messiah who would save us from sin. Everyone who believes in Jesus will live forever with God.

Discussion & Bible skills (10 minutes)

- Bibles, 1 per kid
- Story Point Poster
- Small Group Timeline and Map Set (005802970, optional)

Distribute a Bible to each kid. Help kids find John 3. You may display the New Testament Israel Map to show the kids where Jerusalem is. (*H5*) Ask a strong reader to read John 3:1-6, 14-18 aloud. Remind the kids that the Book of John was written by Jesus' disciple and friend John, not John the Baptist.

Ask the following questions. Lead the group to discuss:

Option: Retell or review the Bible story using the bolded text of the Bible story script.

1. How did Nicodemus know that Jesus had been sent by God? (*because of the miracles Jesus performed, John 3:2*)

2. What did Jesus say must happen for a person to see the kingdom of God? (*The person must be born again, or born of the Spirit; John 3:3-6*)

3. Jesus said that He had been sent by God not to punish the world, but to do what? (*save the world, John 3:17*)

4. What does it mean to be born again? *Prompt the kids to think about the ending of their old, sinful lives and the start of their new lives in Jesus. Remind them that God declares sinners righteous when they believe in Jesus. God no longer sees believers as sinners, but as saints. Our new and eternal life with God starts as soon as we believe the gospel.*

5. What does it mean to have eternal life? *Discuss the idea that eternal life with God is not just regular life that never ends, but joyful, loving, obedient life that goes on forever. A believer's new life begins right away. Even after physical death, our souls live with God forever. When Jesus returns, we will continue living with God in glorified bodies.*

6. Why did God send Jesus to save us? *Remind the kids that God loves people and always does what is for His glory and our good. We are special to God, and He wanted to save us from sin to show His goodness and love.*

SAY • **Jesus taught that we must be born again**. God wants us to believe the gospel so we can have a personal relationship with Him forever.

LOW PREP

· construction paper
· marker
· tape (optional)

Activity choice (10 minutes)

OPTION 1: Stick to the plan

Write the following phrases on separate sheets of construction paper. Place the sheets on the floor around your room. You may choose to secure the sheets in place using tape.

1. Make friends.
2. Eat a meal together.
3. Explore the city.
4. Invite friends to your home.
5. Give them a Bible.
6. Talk about Jesus.
7. Pray for them.
8. Invite them to church.
9. Enjoy their company.
10. Tell them how to become a Christian.

Lead the kids from sheet to sheet to discuss each step in this evangelism plan. Talk about ways they might accomplish each step.

SAY • Missionaries like Heiden and Neena Ratner in Las Vegas, Nevada, are leading people to Jesus. Those steps were an example how someone might lead a person to Jesus. We can do those things, too! **Jesus taught that we must be born again**. When we help people come to know Jesus, we are helping them begin their new life as a Christian.

Tip: Use this activity option to reinforce the missions moment found in Teach the Story.

OPTION 2: Bubble pop

Form two teams of kids. Provide each team with a bottle of bubbles, including a bubble wand. The players of each team will take turns blowing a bubble and catching it on the bubble wand. Time how long the bubbles last. Whichever

· bubble solution and wands, 1 set per team
· stopwatch

team has the longest lasting bubble earns a point. Play additional rounds. After each player on both teams has a chance to blow and catch a bubble, add up the scores and declare the team with the most points the winners.

SAY • It was really hard to make a bubble last. It was here only for a moment before it popped. In a way, that reminds us of our lives on earth. In the big picture, our lives on earth are pretty short.

However, when we believe in Jesus, we inherit everlasting life with God. No matter how short our present lives might be, we will still live forever with God. **Jesus taught that we must be born again** to experience everlasting life.

Reflection and prayer (5 minutes)

Distribute a sheet of paper to each child. Ask the kids to write about or draw a picture to answer the following questions:

· pencils and crayons
· paper
· Bible Story Coloring Page, 1 per kid

• What does this story teach me about God or about the gospel?
• What does this story teach me about myself?
• Whom can I tell about this story?

Make sure to send the sheets home with kids alongside the activity page so that parents can see what their kids have been learning.

If time remains, take prayer requests or allow kids to complete the Bible story coloring page provided with this session. Pray for your group.

Tip: Give parents this week's *Big Picture Cards for Families* to allow families to interact with the biblical content at home.

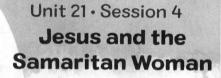

Use Week of:

Unit 21 · Session 4
Jesus and the Samaritan Woman

BIBLE PASSAGE:
John 4

STORY POINT:
Jesus gives the Holy Spirit
to those who believe.

KEY PASSAGE:
John 3:16

BIG PICTURE QUESTION:
What makes people special?
People are special because we are
made in God's image, as male
and female, to know Him.

INTRODUCE THE STORY	TEACH THE STORY	APPLY THE STORY
(10–15 MINUTES)	(25–30 MINUTES)	(25–30 MINUTES)
PAGE 214	**PAGE 216**	**PAGE 222**

 → →

Additional resources are available at gospelproject.com. For free training and session-by-session help, visit MinistryGrid.com/thegospelproject.

LEADER Bible Study

At the time Jesus was on earth, Jews and Samaritans didn't get along. The strife between the two groups stretched back hundreds of years, to the Babylonian exile.

When the Babylonians attacked Judah, they moved a large group of God's people away from their homes. But some of the people—the poorest, sickest, least able to work—were left behind in the region that became known as Samaria. The exile lasted 70 years. During that time, those left in Samaria began to mingle with their neighbors to the north. They intermarried and practiced foreign customs. While the Samaritans still believed in God, they adapted foreign beliefs as well.

The Jews who returned home from Babylon to rebuild God's temple in Jerusalem rejected this new way of life. They were dedicated to obeying and worshiping God, so they didn't agree with the Samaritans' practices. The Samaritans opposed the Jews' efforts to reestablish their nation. In time, the Jews' hate for the Samaritans grew—so much so that a Jew traveling from Judea to Galilee would take a longer route to travel around Samaria rather than through it.

Jesus broke down barriers when He traveled to Galilee by way of Samaria. Even more surprising, Jesus stopped at a well around noon and asked a Samaritan woman for a drink. Jewish men did not speak to women in public.

But Jesus was kind to her, and He offered her a gift: living water. The woman didn't understand, but Jesus revealed His knowledge of her past. He even gave her a glimpse of the future. The Samaritan woman expected a Messiah to come and fix everything. Jesus said, "I am He."

Explain to kids that the living water Jesus offers is the Holy Spirit. (See John 7:37-39.) The Holy Spirit is a gift that He is eager to give us when we ask Him. Those who receive His grace will never be thirsty again.

The BIBLE Story

Jesus and the Samaritan Woman
John 4

Jesus had been teaching in Judea. He **and His disciples** began traveling back to Galilee. They **traveled through Samaria and stopped in a town with a well. Jesus' disciples went into town to buy food. While Jesus was at the well, a Samaritan woman came to get water from the well. Jesus said to her, "Give Me a drink."**

The woman was surprised. **"Why are You talking to me?"** she asked. **"You're a Jew, and I'm a Samaritan."**

Jesus said, **"I asked you for a drink. You don't know who I am. If you did, you would have asked Me for a drink, and I would give you living water."**

The woman was confused. She **said, "Sir, this well is deep, and You don't have a bucket. Where do You get this 'living water'?"**

Jesus said, **"Anyone who drinks this well water will be thirsty again, but whoever drinks from the water I give will never be thirsty again! In fact, the water I give will become a well inside you, and you will have eternal life."** Jesus was talking about the Holy Spirit, but the woman did not understand.

"Sir," she said, **"give me this water. If I'm not thirsty, I won't have**

to keep coming to this well to get water."

"Go get your husband," Jesus said.

"I don't have a husband," the woman replied.

Jesus knew she was telling the truth. He said, "You don't have a husband now, but you've had five husbands."

Jesus was right. "I see You are a prophet," the woman said. Maybe this prophet could explain something to her. She said, "The Samaritans worship here on a mountain, but the Jews say we need to worship at the temple in Jerusalem."

Jesus said, "Soon you will not need to be in either of those places to worship God in spirit and in truth."

The woman said, "I know the Messiah is coming. When He comes, He will explain everything to us."

Then Jesus said, "I am the Messiah."

The woman left and told the people in her town, "Come, see a man who told me everything I ever did! Could this be the Messiah?"

Many Samaritans believed in Jesus because of what the woman said. Jesus stayed in their town for two days. **Many more believed because of what Jesus said. They told the woman, "We no longer believe because of what you said, for we have heard for ourselves and know that this really is the Savior of the world."**

Christ Connection: Jesus offers something better than physical water; He gives us Himself. Jesus gives the Holy Spirit to everyone who comes to Him by faith. We can worship Him as Lord and Savior wherever we are.

Bible Storytelling Tips

- **Use props:** Carry a bucket or water jug as you tell the Bible story.
- **Display a map:** Show a Bible times map and point out the locations of Judea, Galilee, and Samaria. Consider using the New Testament Israel Map from the Small Group Timeline and Map Set (005802970).

INTRODUCE the Story

SESSION TITLE: Jesus and the Samaritan Woman
BIBLE PASSAGE: John 4
STORY POINT: Jesus gives the Holy Spirit to those who believe.
KEY PASSAGE: John 3:16
BIG PICTURE QUESTION: What makes people special? People are special because we are made in God's image, as male and female, to know Him.

Welcome time

Greet each kid as he or she arrives. Use this time to collect the offering, fill out attendance sheets, and help new kids connect to your group. Prompt kids to share what their favorite beverages are.

SAY • No matter what your favorite drink is, many people agree that clean water is one of the healthiest things we can drink. Our bodies need water to live, and because it doesn't have any calories, sugar, or sweeteners, it's considered a lot healthier than sodas or juice. Today we will learn about a special kind of water that only Jesus can give, and it's the best of all.

Activity page (5 minutes)

· "Well Wares" activity page, 1 per kid
· pencils or markers

Invite kids to complete the "Well Wares" activity page. Instruct the kids to circle all the items a person could use to drink water from the well. They will find three jugs, one bucket, and ten cups.

SAY • Today we will learn about a very special talk Jesus had with a woman He met at a well in Samaria. What might Jesus have told her?

Session starter (10 minutes)

OPTION 1: Everything you did

Instruct the kids to sit on the floor. Select a volunteer to come in front of the other kids and act out something she did the day before. Allow the rest of the group to guess what she is acting out. Whoever is correct will take the next turn acting out something he did.

SAY • We do all kinds of things in a day. Some things might be easy for another to guess, such as eating or sleeping, but other things might be hard to guess. Today we will hear a story about a time Jesus showed He knew about a person's sin without her telling Him.

OPTION 2: Watercolors

Provide each kid with paper and a paintbrush. Instruct kids to share the watercolors and to dip their brushes in a cup of water between using any two colors. Give them time to paint a picture of whatever they would like to paint. You may wish to provide smocks or oversized T-shirts or to protect clothing.

- paper
- watercolor paints
- paintbrushes, 1 per kid
- cups
- water
- paper towels for cleanup
- smocks or oversized T-shirts to protect clothing (optional)

SAY • Those colors are beautiful, but they didn't really work as paint until we added water to them. Today we will learn about a kind of water Jesus said He would add to our lives to allow us to live for Him.

Transition to teach the story

TEACH the Story

SESSION TITLE: Jesus and the Samaritan Woman
BIBLE PASSAGE: John 4
STORY POINT: Jesus gives the Holy Spirit to those who believe.
KEY PASSAGE: John 3:16
BIG PICTURE QUESTION: What makes people special? People are special because we are made in God's image, as male and female, to know Him.

Countdown

· countdown video

Show the countdown video as you transition to teach the story. Set it to end as the session begins.

Introduce the session (3 minutes)

· leader attire
· first aid kit

[Leader enters wearing navy blue cargo pants and a short-sleeve white button-down. He or she is carrying a first aid kit.]

Tip: If you prefer not to use themed content or characters, adapt or omit this introduction.

LEADER • Hey there, folks! I'm glad to see you. I just got done admitting a man into the hospital with severe heatstroke. As the weather gets warmer, it is growing more and more important to take precautions if you know you're going to be outside for a long time. This poor gentleman was working on getting his yard all ready for the summer months, and he forgot almost all of the important steps necessary to be safe in hot weather.

It's important to protect your skin and eyes with sunblock and sunglasses. It's also important to wear cool, breathable clothing. A nice, wide-brimmed hat to keep the sun off your face is always a good idea too. And most importantly, you need to drink lots of water. Many times, we don't realize just how much fluid we lose to sweat. It's important to rehydrate yourself when you are having fun in the sun. Some experts say that an adult should drink around two liters, nearly half a gallon, each day—maybe even more if you will be working hard in the sun. Now, for you kids, that would likely be too much water, but my point is you should stay hydrated in the heat.

You know, it reminds me of a Bible story. Let me tell you about the time Jesus was thirsty and met a woman who needed water even more than He did. But not regular water, living water!

Big picture question (1 minute)

LEADER • As we hear this story, I want you to remember the big picture question and answer. *What makes people special? People are special because we are made in God's image, as male and female, to know Him.* That means that God loves each of us uniquely. He wants all of us to be saved by trusting Jesus. He wants to have a loving relationship with us as our heavenly Father. No other created thing is described as "made in God's image." Only humans carry that extra special distinction.

Giant timeline (1 minute)

Show the giant timeline. Point to individual Bible stories as you review.

· Giant Timeline

LEADER • Jesus' public ministry was under way. **People came to Jesus and He healed them. Jesus taught that He is the Messiah**, but some still rejected Him. **Jesus taught that we must be born again**. Let's hear what else He taught.

Tell the Bible story (10 minutes)

- Bibles
- "Jesus and the Samaritan Woman" video
- Big Picture Question Poster
- Bible Story Picture Poster
- Story Point Poster

Open your Bible to John 4. Use the Bible storytelling tips on the Bible story page to help you tell the story, or show the Bible story video "Jesus and the Samaritan Woman."

LEADER • Jesus stopped to talk to a woman, which was a bit strange in those days. More than that, she was a Samaritan; the Samaritans and the Jews did not get along well. Many years before, when the Northern Kingdom of Israel was conquered by Assyria, some of the people living in Samaria—their capital—did not get taken away. However, most of those people did not obey God; they married people who worshiped false gods. As a result, the Jewish people who came back from Babylon did not like the disobedient Samaritans who were still living in the land.

Jesus loved the Samaritan woman though. He was not bothered that she was a woman or that she was a Samaritan; she was special to God. *What makes people special? People are special because we are made in God's image, as male and female, to know Him*.

Jesus knew all about the woman's sin and still wanted to know her and save her. He talked about living water, but she was confused. He didn't mean literal water, He meant the Holy Spirit. **Jesus gives the Holy Spirit to those who believe**. The Holy Spirit lives inside believers, and He helps us to understand God's Word and obey Him.

When we have the Holy Spirit living within us, love and joy begin to fill our lives and overflow into the lives of the people around us. We become like a new well that can provide refreshment to our friends, family, and everyone we meet. If we tell them the good news about Jesus, and they believe, they will be filled with the Holy Spirit also! In that way, it is almost like our "living water" can transfer into the lives of others.

Christ connection

LEADER • Jesus offers something better than physical water; He gives us Himself. Jesus gives the Holy Spirit to everyone who comes to Him by faith. We can worship Him as Lord and Savior wherever we are. We can spread the good news about Jesus and help other people begin a relationship with Him. Then they can be filled with living water too!

Note: You may use this opportunity to use Scripture and the guide provided to explain how to become a Christian. Make sure kids know when and where they can ask questions.

Questions from kids video (3 minutes)

Show the "Unit 21, Session 4" questions from kids video. Prompt kids to think about how they can share the gospel with someone they may not have anything in common with. Guide them to discuss ways they can show the love of Jesus to everyone they meet this week.

· "Unit 21, Session 4" Questions from Kids video

Missions moment (3 minutes)

Display the "Walk Church in Prayer" printable and ask a volunteer to read the caption. Stop and pray, or ask for a volunteer to pray according to the provided prompt.

· "Walk Church in Prayer" printable

LEADER • The Ratners and the Christians at Walk Church believe in the power of prayer and that the Holy Spirit will help them share Jesus with more people. **Jesus gives the Holy Spirit to those who believe**. Let's pray that the Holy Spirit will help the Ratners and missionaries all over the world.

Key passage (5 minutes)

· Key Passage Poster
· "In This Way (John 3:16)" song

Show the key passage poster. Lead the boys and girls to read together John 3:16. Then sing "In This Way (John 3:16)."

LEADER • Our key passage reminds us that God displayed His love for us in a very amazing way. God sent Jesus to die on the cross for our sins. Everyone who believes in Jesus will be saved from sin and live forever with God.

Sing (4 minutes)

· "Take It to the Lord" song

LEADER • Jesus loves us no mater who we are or what we have done. He wants everyone to know God, experience forgiveness, and be free from sin. He is the greatest friend we could have.

Sing together "Take It to the Lord."

Pray (2 minutes)

Invite kids to pray before dismissing to apply the story.

LEADER • Father, thank You for sending Jesus. We cannot earn Your love, and we praise You for loving us anyway. Help us love others with love that overflows from You. Give us wisdom and courage to share the gospel with those around us. Amen.

Dismiss to apply the story

The Gospel: God's Plan for Me

Ask kids if they have ever heard the word *gospel*. Clarify that the word *gospel* means "good news." It is the message about Christ, the kingdom of God, and salvation. Use the following guide to share the gospel with kids.

God rules. Explain to kids that the Bible tells us God created everything, and He is in charge of everything. Invite a volunteer to read Genesis 1:1 from the Bible. Read Revelation 4:11 or Colossians 1:16-17 aloud and explain what these verses mean.

We sinned. Tell kids that since the time of Adam and Eve, everyone has chosen to disobey God. (Romans 3:23) The Bible calls this sin. Because God is holy, God cannot be around sin. Sin separates us from God and deserves God's punishment of death. (Romans 6:23)

God provided. Choose a child to read John 3:16 aloud. Say that God sent His Son, Jesus, the perfect solution to our sin problem, to rescue us from the punishment we deserve. It's something we, as sinners, could never earn on our own. Jesus alone saves us. Read and explain Ephesians 2:8-9.

Jesus gives. Share with kids that Jesus lived a perfect life, died on the cross for our sins, and rose again. Because Jesus gave up His life for us, we can be welcomed into God's family for eternity. This is the best gift ever! Read Romans 5:8; 2 Corinthians 5:21; or 1 Peter 3:18.

We respond. Tell kids that they can respond to Jesus. Read Romans 10:9-10,13. Review these aspects of our response: Believe in your heart that Jesus alone saves you through what He's already done on the cross. Repent, turning from self and sin to Jesus. Tell God and others that your faith is in Jesus.

Offer to talk with any child who is interested in responding to Jesus. Provide *I'm a Christian Now!* for new Christians to take home and complete with their families.

APPLY the Story

SESSION TITLE: Jesus and the Samaritan Woman
BIBLE PASSAGE: John 4
STORY POINT: Jesus gives the Holy Spirit to those who believe.
KEY PASSAGE: John 3:16
BIG PICTURE QUESTION: What makes people special? People are special because we are made in God's image, as male and female, to know Him.

Key passage activity (5 minutes)

- Key Passage Poster
- marker
- plastic cups

Before the session, write each word or phrase of the key passage on a separate plastic cup. Invite volunteers to say the key passage from memory. Thank each kid for her efforts and encourage all the kids to keep working to memorize the verse. Then, provide the cups to the group and challenge them to work together to put the key passage in order.

SAY • God didn't just say He loves us, He showed it. God proved His love by His plan to send Jesus to die for us and make the way to have forgiveness and eternal life. Our key passage reminds us that we don't have to do anything to earn this amazing gift. As soon as we believe the gospel, we get eternal life!

Discussion & Bible skills (10 minutes)

- Bibles, 1 per kid
- Story Point Poster
- Small Group Timeline and Map Set (005802970, optional)

Distribute a Bible to each kid. Help kids find John 4. Briefly review how to use the table of contents to find books of the Bible, and remind kids that the large numbers mark the different chapters, while the small numbers separate each chapter into different verses. Consider showing the New Testament Israel Map to help kids understand where Samaria is. (*F4*)

Ask the following questions. Lead the group to discuss:

Option: Retell or review the Bible story using the bolded text of the Bible story script.

1. What did Jesus ask for when He first saw the Samaritan woman? (*a drink of water, John 4:7*)

2. What did Jesus say would happen to a person who drinks the living water? (*He will never thirst again. It will become a well in him. He will have eternal life; John 4:14*)

3. Where did Jesus say people will worship God? (*anywhere, in spirit and truth; John 4:23-24*)

4. What is the living water Jesus spoke about? *Guide kids to see that the living water is a picture of what the Holy Spirit is like. When we believe the gospel, Jesus sends the Holy Spirit to live within us. He helps us to love and obey God and fills our lives with joy and love so that we can "overflow" joy and love onto other people.*

5. What does it mean to worship God in spirit and in truth? *Discuss how everyone worships* something, *but only believers worship the one true God. Point out that worshiping in spirit means that our very core, including our emotions, is involved in worshiping God. Explain that worshiping in truth means we worship the true God when we understand the wonderful truth of what He has done for us.*

6. How can we receive "living water"? *Remind the kids that the Bible teaches everyone who believes the gospel will be saved. Help them understand that when we believe the gospel, we repent of sin and love God. God forgives our sin, gives us new hearts, and sends the Holy Spirit to live in us and help us obey God out of love.*

SAY • **Jesus gives the Holy Spirit to those who believe**. Anyone can be a believer because Jesus loves all people. The gift of salvation is freely offered to us.

Activity choice (10 minutes)

OPTION 1: Prayer map

Display a map of the United States. Distribute sticky notes and crayons. Invite kids to think of ways they can pray for Christians at Walk Church and other Christians who are sharing the gospel in Nevada. Ask kids to write their prayer requests on the sticky notes or draw a picture representing that request. For example, a kid might draw a Bible to represent prayers that more people will learn about the Bible. Allow each kid to tape a piece of yarn from your state to Nevada. Then add the sticky note. Take time to pray for missionaries, asking volunteers to pray aloud.

SAY • Praying is a very important and powerful way that we support missionaries and churches around the world. That's why people ask us to please pray for them. They know that our prayers matter!

Consider leaving the map displayed in your room for a few weeks to remind kids to pray for missionaries.

OPTION 2: Blessing overflow

Provide a sheet of paper and a pencil to each kid. Ask kids to write about or draw pictures of a few things they consider to be blessings. Help them think through things like their families, their school, their friends, their church family, and so forth. Then challenge the kids to wad their papers into balls and toss them into the cup. Allow them a few chances, or they may simply place their paper wad in the cup. By the end, the cup should be overflowing with paper wads.

SAY • God blesses us in so many ways. It is good to remember the blessings we have from God. The Bible teaches that every good gift is from God. The best gift we could receive is salvation from sin. **Jesus**

- map of the United States
- yarn
- sticky notes
- crayons
- tape

Tip: Use this activity option to reinforce the missions moment found in Teach the Story.

LOW PREP

- plastic cup
- paper
- pencils